FLORA: *A BIOGRAPHY*

Flora MacDonald, 1747

PORTRAIT BY RICHARD WILSON

FLORA

A BIOGRAPHY

by *ELIZABETH GRAY VINING*

J. B. LIPPINCOTT COMPANY

Philadelphia & New York

TO MY SISTER
WITH LOVE

PREFACE

NO child with a Scottish father could fail to have heard the story of Flora MacDonald, the Highland lass who helped Bonnie Prince Charlie to escape when he was being hunted through the Highlands and islands with a price of thirty thousand pounds on his head. I was nearly grown up, however, before I learned that Flora had later come to North Carolina and got herself involved in our Revolution — and on the wrong side, at that. In 1930, when I was married and living in North Carolina, I wrote a book for children, *Meggy MacIntosh*, in which Flora appeared as an important character. While I was doing the research for it, I discovered how little had been written about her and how larded with legend that little was, and I resolved that some day I would write the true story of her life.

Biographies of her can be counted on the fingers of one hand. The first (1870) was a highly fictitious *Autobiography* written by "A Granddaughter." William Jolly's *Flora Mac-Donald in Uist* (1886) and J. P. MacLean's *Flora MacDonald in America* (1909) are useful, if not always dependable, for parts of her life. The Reverend Alexander MacGregor wrote in 1882 a little book that went unrevised into numerous editions, which is full of errors and decorated with pious observations more appreciated in his period than in ours. Though this long served, *faute de mieux,* as the standard biography and was the basis of the account of Flora in the *Dictionary of National Biography,* much the best book about her, now out of print, appeared in 1938: *The Truth about Flora MacDonald* by Allan Reginald MacDonald, who was, so the Preface states, a great-great-grandson of Flora's second cousin. Mr. MacDonald had spent many years gathering material for this book, which is studded with carefully documented facts. He died before he had quite finished it and Dr. Donald MacKinnon, then Presbyterian minister of Portree,

9

Skye, completed and edited it. This has been invaluable and my own book could scarcely have been written without it, but as neither Mr. MacDonald nor Dr. MacKinnon had been in North Carolina or had access to the North Carolina material, that part of the book is meager and sometimes inaccurate.

The search for Flora MacDonald has taken me three times to Skye; to Edinburgh, for the National Library of Scotland; to London, for the Public Record Office; to Washington, D.C., for the National Archives; and, of course, to North Carolina. I have been fortunate in being able to meet and talk with Dr. MacKinnon in Kirkcaldy, Fife, where he now lives, and with those two devoted North Carolina antiquarians, Mr. Rassie Wicker of Pinehurst and Mr. Malcolm Fowler of Lillington, who have spent much of their lives tracking down the forgotten places associated with Flora MacDonald, combing old deeds and tax records and walking the tangled creek beds in search of ruins. I am grateful to all three of these gentlemen for their help. I should like to thank also Dr. Christopher Crittenden, Director of the Department of Archives and History of North Carolina, and members of his staff; Mr. V. S. Ritchie of the Manuscript Division of the National Library of Scotland and his assistants; the staffs of the Public Record Office in London, of the Carolina Room of the Library of the University of North Carolina, of Swarthmore College and of the Library of the Pennsylvania Historical Society, Philadelphia. My sister, Violet Gordon Gray, has contributed unstinted interest and encouragement and accompanied me on the first and the last of my trips to Scotland, just thirty years apart.

CONTENTS

Preface	PAGE	9
A Key to the MacDonalds and MacLeods		15
1. Girlhood in South Uist		19
2. The 'Forty-five		29
3. Flora to the Rescue		45
4. Over the Sea to Skye		60
5. The Arrests		71
6. Prisoner		83
7. Marriage		97
8. The Family Grows		105
9. Emigration Fever		113
10. Distinguished Visitors		121
11. Going to Seek a Fortune in North Carolina		129
12. The New Home		135
13. The Highlanders Take Sides		146
14. The Battle of Moore's Creek Bridge		160
15. Aftermath		168
16. Allan's Adventures		173
17. Back to Skye		181
18. The Closing Years		188
Notes		199

LIST OF ILLUSTRATIONS

FLORA MacDONALD, 1747   FRONTISPIECE
    Portrait by Richard Wilson

                                      FACING PAGE
CHARLES EDWARD STUART, *The Young Prince*   64
    Portrait by Maurice de la Tour

ANNE *and* ALLAN MacDONALD   65

THE DUKE OF CUMBERLAND   96
    Portrait by Sir Joshua Reynolds

CHARLES EDWARD STUART *in his old age*   97
    Portrait by H. D. Hamilton

13

Maps

PAGE

OUTER HEBRIDES 21

SKYE 26

ITINERARY of Prince Charles, Flora, O'Neil and
MacEachain, June 20–July 1, 1746 47

EASTERN NORTH CAROLINA 137

14

A Key to the MacDonalds and MacLeods

Note on the spelling of the name MacDonald: Modern usage tends to prefer Macdonald. Flora herself and her husband spelled it McDonald. Dr. Donald MacKinnon, however, informed me that the correct spelling in Scotland is MacDonald, and that only names derived from churchly callings, such as Macnab (from abbot) should be spelled with a small letter following the Mac.

Flora MacDonald, the protectress of Prince Charles Edward Stuart

Alexander MacDonald, Flora's second son

Alexander MacDonald of Boisdale, half brother of Clanranald (see below), friend to Prince Charles

Alexander MacDonald of Cuidreach, husband of Flora's half sister Annabella

Alexander MacDonald of Kingsburgh, chief factor to Sir Alexander MacDonald of Sleat and tacksman of Kingsburgh, father-in-law of Flora

Sir Alexander MacDonald of Sleat, seventh baronet, chief of the MacDonalds of Sleat; Mugstot was his home

Sir Alexander MacDonald of Sleat, ninth baronet, son of the seventh baronet; succeeded his elder brother James as chief

Alexander MacDonald of Staten Island, captain in the 84th, or Royal Highland Emigrants, Regiment, cousin of Allan MacDonald

Allan MacDonald of Kingsburgh, Flora's husband

Father Allan MacDonald, chaplain to Prince Charles

Angus MacDonald, Flora's grandfather

Annabella MacDonald, Flora's half sister, wife of Alexander MacDonald of Cuidreach

Anne MacDonald, Flora's daughter, wife of Alexander MacLeod (see below)

Charles MacDonald, Flora's eldest son

Donald MacDonald, son of Annabella and Alexander Mac-
Donald of Cuidreach; married Flora's daughter
Fanny

General Donald MacDonald of the North Carolina Highlanders

Donald Roy MacDonald, captain in the Prince's army, half
brother of Hugh MacDonald of Baleshare (see below)

Elizabeth MacDonald of Largie, Flora's cousin

Frances MacDonald, "Fanny," Flora's second daughter and
youngest child; married Annabella's son Donald

Hugh MacDonald of Armadale, Flora's stepfather

Hugh MacDonald of Baleshare, friend of Prince Charles,
half brother of Donald Roy MacDonald

Jacques Étienne Joseph Alexandre MacDonald, son of Neil
MacEachain MacDonald; became Napoleon's Marshal
MacDonald, Duc de Tarentum

James MacDonald, half brother of Flora MacDonald

James MacDonald, Flora's fourth son, lieutenant in the
North Carolina Highlanders, captain in Tarleton's
British Legion; later known as Captain MacDonald of
Flodigarry

James MacDonald, lieutenant in the North Carolina Highlanders, brother of Alexander MacDonald of Cuidreach

Sir James MacDonald of Sleat, eighth baronet, succeeded his
father, Sir Alexander, as chief of the MacDonalds of
Sleat

John MacDonald, Flora's youngest son

Kenneth MacDonald, aide-de-camp to General Donald Mac-
Donald, brother of Alexander MacDonald of Cuidreach

Margaret MacDonald, "Peggy," daughter of Ranald Mac-
Donald of Clanranald and Lady Clanranald

16

A Key to the MacDonalds and MacLeods

Lady Margaret MacDonald, wife of the first Sir Alexander MacDonald of Sleat, daughter of Lord Eglinton

Lady MacDonald, wife of the younger Sir Alexander Mac-Donald of Sleat

Marion MacDonald, Flora's mother, who married (1) Ranald MacDonald of Milton and (2) Hugh MacDonald of Armadale

Neil MacEachain MacDonald, possibly a cousin of Flora's, staunch friend of Prince Charles

Ranald MacDonald of Milton, Flora's father

Ranald MacDonald, Flora's brother, who died young

Ranald MacDonald, Flora's third son

Ranald MacDonald of Clanranald, chief of the MacDonalds of Clanranald

Ranald MacDonald, "young Clanranald," eldest son of the chief

Alexander MacLeod, Flora's son-in-law, husband of Anne, illegitimate son of Norman MacLeod of MacLeod

Donald MacLeod, colonel of the North Carolina Highlanders, killed at the Battle of Moore's Creek Bridge

Donald MacLeod of Galtergill, faithful boatman to Prince Charles

Lieutenant John MacLeod of the MacLeod Militia; questioned Flora at Dunvegan

Captain John MacLeod of Talisker, of the MacLeod Militia, tacksman of Talisker

Malcolm MacLeod of Brea, Raasay, Captain in the Prince's army and friend of the Prince

Dr. Murdoch MacLeod of Cross Creek, North Carolina, surgeon to the North Carolina Highlanders

Norman MacLeod of MacLeod, chief of Clan MacLeod; lived at Dunvegan Castle

Norman MacLeod of MacLeod, the younger; succeeded his grandfather as chief

Girlhood in South Uist

OFF the west coast of Scotland lie the Hebrides, a group of more than five hundred islands, deeply probed by fingers of the sea, spiked with mountains, swathed in mist; islands of fierce winds and drenching rains, of sudden sunshine; of harsh history and tender songs; of sea birds and shaggy cattle, of peat smoke and barren soil; of rugged men — soldiers, fishermen, farmers — and women whose especial qualities are blitheness and tranquility.

The Inner Hebrides are more accessible and easily known: Skye, which is the largest, Rum, Eigg, Jura, Iona and others. The Outer Hebrides lie across bodies of water called the Minch, the Little Minch and the Sea of the Hebrides; known collectively as the Long Island, they are a thin string of islands extending a hundred and thirty miles from the Butt of Lewis in the north to Barra Head in the south. Beyond the Outer Hebrides stretches the Atlantic Ocean, with nothing between them and the coast of Labrador but the tiny isle of St. Kilda.

South of Harris and north of Barra in the Long Island are three islands, which are separated by fords passable at low tide: North Uist (pronounced Yew-ist), Benbecula and South Uist, something over forty miles long in all and thirteen miles wide at the widest part. South Uist, the largest of the three, has a spine of mountains running down its length, slightly east of center, of which Ben More, the highest, has an altitude of two thousand feet. The eastern shore beneath the mountains is deeply indented with sea

lochs. On the western side is the *machair,* a wide belt of low
and level sandy ground covered with grass and wildflowers
between the hills and the Atlantic Ocean.

Here, on a farm called Milton, Flora MacDonald was
born in 1722. Flora's father, Ranald MacDonald, was the
tacksman of Milton and Ballivanoch, another farm in Benbecula. That is to say, he received large grants of land or
"tacks" from his chief, who was his cousin, which he partly
farmed himself and partly rented out to smaller farmers. He
was a gentleman. In the simple but rigid social structure of
the Scottish Highlands in the early eighteenth century the
chiefs, the tacksmen and the clergy were gentlemen; the rest
were the clansmen or "the common Highlanders."

Flora's mother, Marion MacDonald, Ranald's second
wife, was the daughter of the Reverend Angus MacDonald,
the minister of South Uist, known and respected as "the
strong minister" for both his physical and his moral strength,
and Elizabeth MacDonald, daughter of Angus MacDonald
of Largie, in Kintyre. Because there were so many Mac-
Donalds belonging to the five main branches of the great
Clan Donald, and because most of them married MacDonalds and had the same Christian names as well as the same
surname, the only way to keep them straight was the way
the Scots had long ago adopted: by designating individuals
by the name of their estates or tacks. Thus Flora's father was
known as Milton, and Flora herself, even years after her
father's death, as Milton's daughter.

At the time of her birth Europe was temporarily at
peace. The War of the Spanish Succession was over. The
wars of the Austrian Succession, of the Polish Succession
and of Jenkins's Ear, the Seven Years' War, the American
and the French revolutions were still to come. King George I
had been eight years on the throne of Great Britain, having
come to it from Hanover on the death of his first cousin once-
removed, Anne, in accordance with the Act of Settlement of

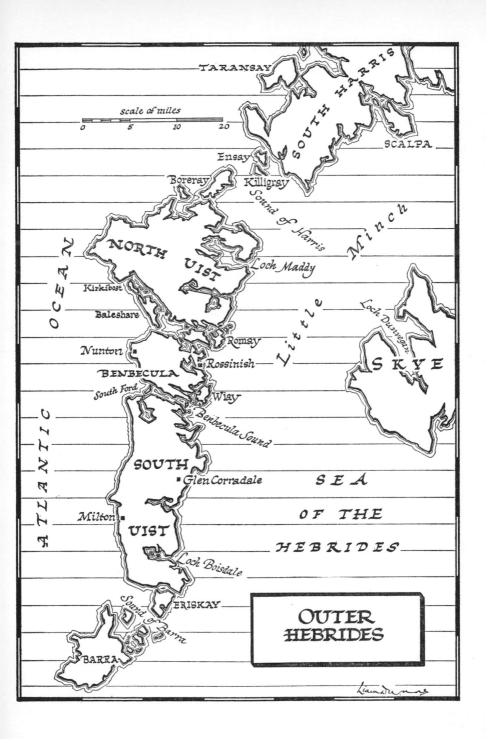

TARANSAY

SOUTH HARRIS

scale of miles

0   5   10   20

SCALPA

Ensay

Boreray Killigray

Sound of Harris

Minch

NORTH UIST

Loch Maddy

OCEAN

Kirkibost

Little

Loch Dunvegan

Baleshare

Romay

Nunton

SKYE

Rossinish

BENBECULA

South Ford

Wiay

Benbecula Sound

SOUTH

SEA

Glen Corradale

OF THE

Milton

UIST

HEBRIDES

Loch Boisdale

ERISKAY

Sound of Barra

OUTER
HEBRIDES

BARRA

ATLANTIC

1701, which ensured England Protestant kings. He was a dull little man who spoke no English and was far more interested in the affairs of Hanover than in those of Britain. The Scots, who had promptly but fruitlessly proclaimed Anne's half brother, James Francis Edward Stuart, King James VIII of Scotland and III of England, sang derisively,

Wha d'ye think we hae gotten for our king
But a wee, wee German lairdie,
And when they went to bring him hame
*He was delvin' in his kail-yairdie.**

James Stuart, "the Old Pretender," son of James II and his second wife, Mary of Modena, was twenty-three years younger than Queen Anne, who was the daughter of the first wife, Anne Hyde. It is not known when James II became a Roman Catholic, but his two daughters, Mary and Anne, brought up as Protestants, married Protestant princes and became queens of England, while his only surviving son, James, a Catholic, was excluded from the succession. James Stuart's first-born son, Charles Edward, later to be known as "the Young Pretender," was two years old in 1722, and George's third and favorite son, William Augustus, Duke of Cumberland, was a year old.

The small Flora MacDonald grew up in South Uist quite unconscious of the way that her destiny was to be shared by those two royal babies so near her own age.

She had two elder brothers, Angus and Ranald. When she was a year old her grandfather, the minister, died on his way back to South Uist from a visit to Largie, and the following year her father, who was of the same age as his father-in-law, also died, leaving Ballivanoch and Milton "well stocked with cattle and sheep."[1] Marion MacDonald was left with two tacks to manage and three young children to bring up alone.

* Kail-yairdie: cabbage patch.

22

Four years later her problem was solved by a masterful young man from Skye. Hugh MacDonald was the third son of the tacksman of Kingsburgh, one of the largest tacks in the possession of his cousin Sir Alexander MacDonald of Sleat. Sir Alexander was chief of the Sleat branch of the MacDonalds and seventh baronet as well, claiming descent from the greatest MacDonald of them all, Somerled, Lord of the Isles. Hugh, like many of the young Highland gentlemen of his century, seeing no future in the barren and overpopulated acres of his homeland, had gone off to serve as an officer in the French army. When he returned minus one eye (no doubt it was during this experience that he had the accident which resulted in his being known as "one-eyed Hugh"), he was at a loss for something to do, until he saw Marion MacDonald struggling with her tacks and her minor children. The traditional story is that he abducted her and carried her off to Armadale in southern Skye, where he had the tack that gave him the name by which he was known, Hugh MacDonald of Armadale. Actually, however, he did not acquire the tack of Armadale until November 4, 1745.[2] He seems rather to have married Marion, moved in with her and managed the farms for his stepson Angus until the boy was of age and capable of taking them over for himself. It has been said that he "acted the part of a faithful husband and stepfather."[3]

Four children were born of Marion's second marriage: Annabella, James and two younger boys.

The house at Milton where they all lived was little more than a cottage, consisting only of three rooms and a kitchen.[4] This was not unusually small even for a tacksman, for houses in the islands were generally simple indeed. Those of the lesser tenants and crofters were no more than a single windowless room with a fireplace in the center and a hole above it to let the smoke out; one end was penned off for the cow. The tacksman's house, small and plain though it

23

might be, was usually well furnished. Dr. Johnson on his visit to the Highlands fifty years later wrote, "The house and furniture are not always nicely suited. We were driven once, by missing a passage, to the hut [i.e., one-storied house] of a gentleman, where, after a very liberal supper, when I was conducted to my chamber, I found an elegant bed of Indian cotton, spread with fine sheets. The accommodation was flattering; I undressed myself, and felt my feet in the mire. The bed stood upon the bare earth, which a long course of rain had softened to a puddle."[5]

However cramped and primitive the house at Milton might have been, it was surrounded by beauty. It stood on a little knoll, with the Atlantic on one side and four lakes within view on the other. The slopes of Sheaval rose behind it, and a little stream ran the mill which gave the farm its Gaelic name, Airidh Mhuillin, the Shieling of the Mill.

Cattle and sheep were the chief crop, with enough barley for whisky, enough oats for bread and porridge. In the summers they drove the cattle up the mountain slopes for pasturage and slept in little huts high among the larks and heather.

Flora had no formal education. There were no towns in the islands, except Stornoway, a fishing village on the northern tip of Lewis; none, indeed, in the highlands of the mainland nearer than Inverness. There was a girls' boarding school in Inverness, but it was too far away and perhaps too expensive. The sons of the chiefs were sent away to school, to Aberdeen or Edinburgh or England, sometimes to France or Italy; sons of tacksmen might go to Inverness or Aberdeen or be taught by the local minister. Daughters for the most part got what they could from their mothers.

It has been often said that Flora was sent to school in Edinburgh by Lady Margaret MacDonald, a pretty story but unfortunately without foundation. When she went to Leith as a prisoner in 1746, she saw Edinburgh in the distance for the first time. The men who knew her then commented that it was amazing that a young woman who had never been out of the islands of South Uist and Skye, except for a visit to Largie, should be so adequate socially.[6]

It has also been said that she shared the governess of Lady Clanranald's daughters, but Clanranald and his wife had eight sons and only one daughter, Margaret, who was seventeen years younger than Flora and was, moreover, educated in Ireland.[7]

Flora learned at home to speak well, like other Scots of her class, without Scottish accent, to sing, to sew, to read, to write after a fashion. She was brought in touch with the best society of the islands.

Ranald MacDonald, the fourteenth laird of Clanranald, was her father's chief. The Clanranalds lived at Nunton in Benbecula, about fifteen miles from Milton. Nunton got its name from an ancient nunnery, on the site of which it had been built. Clanranald himself was a Roman Catholic; his wife, who was known as Lady Clanranald, and affectionately by her friends as "Lady Clan," was a Presbyterian.

Clanranald's half brother, who lived at Loch Boisdale, in South Uist, and the MacDonalds of Kirkibost in North Uist were cousins of Flora's, but probably the most exciting and romantic figure in her girlhood was Lady Margaret Mac-Donald, the wife of her stepfather's chief. When Flora was seventeen, Sir Alexander MacDonald of Sleat married, for his second wife, Lady Margaret Montgomerie, the fourth of the seven beautiful daughters of the Earl and Countess of Eglinton, and brought her home to Mugstot, his house in Skye.

Lady Margaret's mother was the famous Susanna Kennedy, who became at twenty the third wife of the forty-nine-year-old Earl of Eglinton. Her father, troubled because an impecunious young man named Clark wanted to marry his beautiful and elegant six-foot-tall daughter Susanna, had

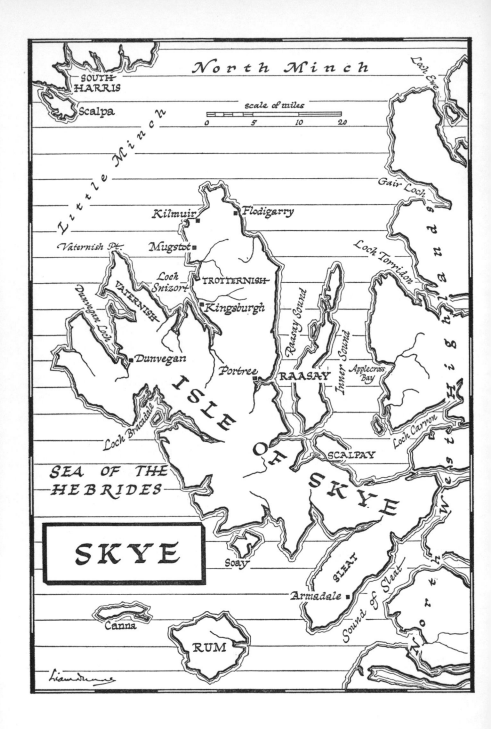

asked the advice of Lord Eglinton. "Bide a wee, Sir Archie," the Earl replied. "My wife's very sickly." Sir Archie bode a wee and his daughter duly became Lady Eglinton. She bore the Earl seven daughters and two sons, and it was said that one of the sights of Edinburgh was "to see the long procession of sedans, containing Lady Eglinton and her seven daughters, devolve from the close and proceed to the Assembly Rooms . . . eight beautiful women conspicuous for their stature and carriage, all dressed in the splendid though formal fashions of that period and inspired at once with dignity of birth and consciousness of beauty."[8]

Lady Margaret, coming to Skye to the rather modest house of Mugstot (Duntulm Castle was in the past, Armadale Castle in the future of the Sleat family) became the darling of her husband's people, loved for her kindness as well as for her beauty and charm. Boswell was told, when he visited Skye in 1773, "that Lady Margaret was quite adored in Skye. That when she rode through the island, the people ran in crowds before her, and took the stones off the road, lest her horse should stumble and she be hurt."[9] There could not have been a great deal of going back and forth between Milton and Skye, but it is evident from Flora's later behavior that she knew and loved Lady Margaret, who must indeed have seemed to the young girl a dazzling figure from the great world.

Some time during Flora's girlhood her brother Ranald lost his life in an accident. There are two versions of the story: one that when he was visiting his cousins on the mainland at Largie, he overstrained himself rowing a boat against a strong wind, burst a blood vessel and died;[10] the other, that he was visiting on the island of Cara, Argyllshire, that he and a young cousin were going out for a day's shooting, that both of them rushed to get the one gun and that in the scuffle the gun went off and killed Ranald.[11] It is impossible

27

to determine now which version is correct. Flora lost a brother.

In 1744, when she was twenty-two, she made her first venture away from the islands and on to the mainland of Scotland; she went to visit her cousins at Largie. It must have been a great occasion for her. The Largie cousins seem to have been rather grand. They had a big house, which was later expanded into a castle, near Campbeltown in Kintyre, that long peninsula that reaches down into the north Irish Channel between Arran and the smaller islands of Islay and Jura. Flora's second cousin, Elizabeth, who was the only child of her father, John MacDonald, the thirteenth of his line to live at Largie, was just about Flora's age. Flora spent ten or eleven months with the Largie family, and perhaps it was then that she acquired the skill at the tea table which was later to evoke admiring comment.

In 1745 her brother Angus, by this time well over twenty-one and married, came into his inheritance of the tacks of Milton and Ballivanoch. Hugh MacDonald then left these farms which he had been managing for his stepson and in November took up, from Sir Alexander MacDonald of Sleat, his cousin and chief, the tack of Armadale in the southern part of Skye, the part of the island with milder air and richer soil, where trees grew and hedges of fuchsias. Flora went with her mother and Hugh and their children, Annabella and James and the two younger boys, to Armadale to live.

Four months earlier, however, an event which was to shake all of their lives had occurred. On July 23, 1745, Prince Charles Edward Stuart landed at Eriskay, a small island off South Uist. He had come to set his father on the throne of Britain.

2

The 'Forty-five

THE two major attempts to put the Stuarts back on the throne are known by their dates, the 'Fifteen and the 'Forty-five. In both cases James Stuart, "the Old Pretender," was the one who was to be re-established. In 1715 the Earl of Mar raised the standard for him and led the rebellion; James appeared briefly in Scotland, but the movement soon collapsed. In 1745 his son Charles Edward, "the Young Pretender," raised the standard for his father and led the troops himself.

The fiasco of the 'Fifteen resulted in the Clan Act, by which every Crown vassal was to forfeit his estates if found guilty of treasonable correspondence with the Pretender, and the Act for Disarming the Highlands, which required all Highlanders to surrender their arms. Those loyal to the government did so at once; the Jacobites turned in rusty and antiquated weapons, hid their good ones and waited for another opportunity. During the thirty years between the two attempts some abortive efforts were made that accomplished nothing but to keep the government wary. Accordingly the English General Wade was sent to build military roads in Scotland, which proved to be of considerable economic advantage to the country. Young Highlanders went away to fight in French or Spanish armies, thereby finding occupation that they enjoyed and getting military training for the next uprising.

Prince Charles Edward Louis Philip Casimir Stuart, the elder son of James Stuart and Clementine Sobieski, a Polish

29

princess, was born in Rome in 1720 and brought up dedicated to the purpose of regaining the throne for his father. To a natural liking for outdoor life he added a determination to prepare himself for his mission. "He loved the wintry woods," wrote Andrew Lang, "hunting, shooting, walking stockingless all to harden himself for the campaigns that lay before his imagination."[1] When he was almost fourteen he had his first taste of the field: he spent two months with the Duke of Liria in a small action in Spain, at which he showed courage and won some popularity with the soldiers.

In 1739 England went to war with Spain in the War of Jenkins's Ear, which was fought actually over trade and sea power and emotionally over the boarding of a British ship by a Spanish naval force and the alleged cutting off of the ear of a British seaman named Robert Jenkins, and it was evident that the other continental powers would sooner or later be involved. Only when England was already preoccupied with war and France disposed to take the opportunity to strike a blow at her through her old ally, Scotland, was there any real chance for the Jacobites. This combination of circumstances appeared in 1740 to be taking shape, and an Association of Six, which included the Duke of Perth, Lord Lovat and Cameron of Lochiel, entered into negotiations with James and the French. If Charles should come with French arms, troops and money, they said, the Highland chiefs would rise.

Early in 1744 the French secretly summoned Charles to Paris to be in readiness while they prepared a formidable expedition against England, consisting of twenty-two warships and 4,000 men, to be followed by an army of 15,000 from Dunkirk. This invasion, however, like some previous invasion attempts, was scattered by storms and came to nothing. Charles lingered on, impatient and unnoticed in Paris.

In May of the following year an English army under the

young Duke of Cumberland was defeated at the Battle of Fontenoy, largely by the Irish Brigade of the French army. It was evident that troops would have to be pulled out of England to fill the gaps in the army in the Low Countries, and to Charles it seemed clear that the moment had come to attack. If the French would not support him, and they made no move to do anything, he would go alone. He managed to borrow from a banker named Walters in Paris 180,000 livres, estimated at four thousand pounds,[2] with which he bought 1,800 broadswords, 20 small fieldpieces, 1,500 muskets and the necessary ammunition. Two Jacobite merchants of Nantes supplied him with two boats, the *Elizabeth* of 64 guns and a brig of 18 guns, *La Doutelle*. With this slender armament, a small remnant of cash and seven men in his train, he sailed from Nantes on June 22, 1745. The seven, who bcame known as the Seven Men of Moidart, were three Scots, an Englishman and three Irishmen. One of the Irishmen was Sir Thomas Sheridan, Charles's tutor, and the members of the crew were told that Charles was Sheridan's son, a student at the Scots College in Paris.

It was an incredible piece of foolhardiness for Charles to set out to overthrow the Hanoverians with seven men and two ships, explainable only by his supreme confidence in his own destiny and his altogether exaggerated notion of the enthusiasm he would arouse in Scotland.

One of his ships he lost almost at once; the *Elizabeth,* which carried most of his arms and supplies, fell foul of an English ship, the *Lion,* was disabled in a sharp engagement and fled back to France. *La Doutelle* escaped through the fog, went on and reached Eriskay on July 23.

The situation in Scotland in 1745 was even less favorable to a successful uprising than it had been in 1715. In 1715 the union of the parliaments of England and Scotland was only eight years old and was still unpopular in Scotland. By 1745, however, prosperity resulting from the union was beginning to make itself felt, though chiefly in the cities of the Lowlands, owing to free trade with England and the colonies. Glasgow had changed from a small university town to a city growing rich from shipbuilding, the manufacturing of linen and the importation of tobacco. The division between Highlands and Lowlands had widened and deepened. To the Lowlander the Gaelic-speaking, cattle-raiding, proud, kilted men of the north were half-clothed, thieving "ruffiens" with "uncowth wappons";[3] to the Highlanders the Sassenachs were moneygrubbers and foreigners. The Highlands themselves were further split between those clans which maintained their Stuart loyalties and those who followed the Campbells under the Duke of Argyll in supporting the government. There was also a fundamental religious difference: the Highland Jacobites were for the most part Roman Catholic or Episcopalian; the Lowlanders and the Campbells were Presbyterian. James had been reared in the Catholic religion and steadily refused to abjure it. Charles in his turn was determinedly Catholic, until 1750; then, when it was too late, he foreswore Catholicism and declared himself a Protestant. In the end, it was the religious question rather than any real love for the Hanoverians that kept the main body of the Scots from supporting the Stuarts. Alexander Carlyle, a Presbyterian minister of Edinburgh born in the same year as Flora MacDonald, wrote in his *Autobiography:* "The commons in general as well as two thirds of the gentry at that period [i.e., 1745] had no aversion to the family of Stuart; and could their religion have been secured, would have been very glad to see them on the throne again."[4]

The geographical line between Highlands and Lowlands ran across Scotland from Moray Firth to Dumbarton in a curve that swelled eastward to take in Stirling, Perth and parts of Aberdeenshire. To the north and west of that line, life was hard, agriculture primitive. Cattle were the chief wealth and cattle raiding, though not the interclan warfare and blood sport it had once been, continued as a means of plundering the Lowlands. The chiefs owned the land. Their younger brothers and cousins had tacks, for which in the past they paid in military service and which they rented out to small farmers, members of the clan who were, or believed themselves to be, of the same blood as the chief. The tacksmen were far better soldiers than farmers and considered themselves superior to work. The land was farmed on the medieval run-rig system, strips parceled out to the tenants. Soil was tilled with a spade. Because of a lack of capital, the risk of increased rents following improvements, the difficulty of organizing drastic cooperative action in a strip system of agriculture and the innate conservatism of both landlords and tenants, there was little if any attempt to improve the barren soil by draining or fertilizing, and the yield was much lower in the Highlands than in the Lowlands, where new methods of farming were beginning to produce results. The animating principle in the Highlands was loyalty to the chiefs, who as well as owning the land and administering justice could call out armies of their own, of which the tacksmen were the officers and the tenants the common soldiers. If the clansmen did not come out willingly, the chiefs did not hesitate to burn their roofs over their heads. The virtues in such a society were hospitality, courage, pride, generosity and a dignity common to all classes. Sir John MacPherson writing to Anne Grant about the civilization of the Highlands at this time, said:

Many causes combined in favor of that state of society, the spirit of true poetry which kept the memory of noble actions, as that of the best affections of the heart, in continued admiration; the hospitality which formed the intercourse of the chiefs and their family connections; the opportunities which the cadets of those families had of seeing foreign countries and serving in the armies of France, Germany and Italy, always to return to their native soil with a good name, together with an emulation between the different clans to surpass each other in acts of liberality and renown. These and other causes gave the manners of the last century in our highlands and islands much of the old early Grecian character mixed with the loyalty and spirit of chivalry.[5]

The Highland chiefs were loyal to the Stuarts, but their loyalty did not blind them to the realities of the situation. They maintained consistently that they would rally to support the Prince only if he came with French money and troops. When he arrived on Eriskay with his seven men and his few remaining livres, there was general consternation.

Clanranald, when he heard the news, exclaimed, "What muckle devil has brought him to this country again?"[6] Clanranald's half brother, Alexander MacDonald of Boisdale in South Uist, who met the Prince on Eriskay, did his best to persuade Charles that this enterprise was doomed to failure; he told him outright that Clanranald would not go in, and even the Seven Men of Moidart urged Charles to give it all up and return to France.

Charles insisted on going on, however, to the mainland of Scotland, landing two days later at Arisaig, on Loch-nan-Uamh opposite the islands of Eigg and Muck. "This wild country," wrote a traveler in 1750, "has always been a Nursery and Sanctuary of Priests. People in general of all Ranks in this barbarous place are much better acquainted with Rome, Madrid and Paris than they are with London or Edinburgh."[7] Borrodale House, where the Prince stayed, was the seat of Aeneas MacDonald, the banker, one of the Seven Men.

The first person to meet the Prince when he set foot on the shore at Arisaig was Flora MacDonald's stepfather, Hugh.

"When the Prince first landed upon the continent of Scotland," Flora told Bishop Forbes in 1747, "Armadale happening to be on the continent was walking on the shore just as the Prince and his friends were sailing toward it." Hugh made inquiries, learned who it was on the French ship. "When the Prince stepped ashore, Armadale was the first man that took him by the hand and kissed it, for he was introduced to the Prince by those who were along with him. The Prince and Armadale conversed some time together. Soon after this Armadale returned to the Isle of Skye and never saw the Prince again, either before or in the time of his skulking."[8]

It is not clear whether or not Armadale was present at the conversations that took place at Borrodale House, but probably he was not. Young Clanranald, "old" Clanranald's eldest son Ranald, was there to tell the Prince that his father would not support him. Charles, however, so captivated the young man that he threw overboard his qualms, promised to lead out his men and engaged to go to Skye and try to gain the support of the two chiefs there, which was vital to the success of any rising.

These chiefs were Sir Alexander MacDonald of Sleat and Norman MacLeod, chief of the MacLeods, who lived in Dunvegan Castle. Though in centuries past the MacDonalds and MacLeods had warred bitterly, the present chiefs, nearly of an age, in their thirties, were close friends. They had been involved in two unsavory episodes that did them no credit, the kidnapping of Lady Grange (at her husband's request) and her imprisonment first on MacDonald's island of Heiskir and later on MacLeod's St. Kilda; and also in a scheme for capturing 100 of their own people and shipping them off to Pennsylvania to be sold as indentured servants. When the ship was discovered at an Irish port the whole story came out, and it was only influence in high places that got the two chiefs out of the mess.

In 1745, MacDonald and MacLeod, conferring hastily, declared that without French troops they could not possibly support the Prince, and they urged prudence on young Clanranald. So far from helping Charles, in fact, the two chiefs acted promptly against him. MacLeod sent word on August 3 to Duncan Forbes, the Lord President of the Sessions, a staunch Whig and Scotland's most enlightened leader, that the Prince had landed, and when Forbes got permission from the government to raise twenty independent companies (that is to say, militia) to put down the Rebellion, MacDonald raised three of the twenty and Mac-Leod four. MacLeod, furthermore, led his men in actual combat on the mainland.

Young Clanranald, however, stood firm. He could not bring with him MacDonalds of his clan from the Long Island, for they were held back by his father and his uncle, but he could and did produce 200 MacDonalds from the mainland. Cameron of Lochiel, the chief of Clan Cameron, promised and delivered 700 more. With the support of these two, Charles decided to go ahead. The crimson and white royal standard was raised at Glenfinnan, at the head of Loch Shiel, and the clans gathered—200 Clanranald MacDonalds, 700 Camerons, 400 MacDonalds of Glengarry, 120 Mac-Donalds of Glencoe, 260 Stewarts of Appin. On the twenty-second of August Charles learned that the government had made an offer of thirty thousand pounds for his head, and he responded promptly by setting the same price on that of the Elector of Hanover. (He had wanted at first to make it, contemptuously, thirty pounds, but was dissuaded.)

As Charles began his successful march to Inverness, Perth and Edinburgh, other clans joined him, until, when he met and defeated General Sir John Cope at the Battle of Prestonpans, near Edinburgh, he had about 2,500 men against Cope's approximately equal number. Cope was better armed and he had drawn up his men in an apparently superior position, with a high wall behind them and a marsh in front. But a native of the district led Charles's army at night by a footpath through the bog; they crept up under cover of the early morning mist, to pounce yelling on the enemy at daybreak. In less than ten minutes of fighting, Cope's infantry was wiped out. Cope himself, at the head of the cavalry, galloped forty miles to Berwick, "the only British general," according to Sir Charles Petrie, "who has been the first to bear the tidings of his own defeat."[9]

This was the year of all his life when Charles Stuart's personal charm was at its height. Alexander Carlyle, not himself a Jacobite, who went to stare at the Prince in Edinburgh, described him thus: "He was a good-looking man, of about five feet ten inches; his hair was dark red and his eyes black. His features were regular, his visage long, much sunburnt and freckled, and his countenance thoughtful and melancholy."[10] The ladies of Edinburgh, even many whose husbands stood firm by the government, went into a state of romantic rapture over him. He was, however, at this stage of his life, much more of a man's man. He appeared at balls looking melancholy and kissed hands, but his mind was in the field.

The subsequent course of the Rebellion of the 'Forty-five can be briefly summarized. From his triumph in Edinburgh Charles marched on to Carlisle and then deep into England. Though many of his Highlanders deserted when they got away from the hills, others had joined him, including some Lowlanders, and he had now somewhere around 5,000 men. By early December he had got as far on his way to the capital as Derby, 128 miles from London. Here he paused for a council of war.

To Charles it seemed that everything lay before him. London was in a state of hysteria and panic and was reported to be full of Jacobites who would welcome him as savior. His advisers, however, pointed out that the English Jacobites in the north had not flocked to his banner as he had expected, that his Highland troops were uneasy so far from home, that the French were still missing, that the Duke of Cumberland, summoned home from France in October, was on his flank with an army twice the size of his, and that Marshal Wade, at Newcastle with 10,000, was waiting to close in on him. On December 6, "Black Friday," he yielded to his generals, and the retreat which was to end four months later on Culloden Moor was begun.

The defeat on April 16 on the desolate, sleet-drenched moor near Inverness was complete. Outnumbered nearly two to one, exhausted by a fruitless night march of twelve miles through hill and bog, torn by internal dissension — for the MacDonalds, deprived of the position on the right wing which they considered their hereditary prerogative, sulked disastrously — the Highlanders entered battle. Twenty-five minutes later they lay dead "in layers of three and four deep,"[11] while the victors with cold brutality went about dragging out and shooting the wounded. One thousand of the Jacobites were killed in the battle or immediately afterwards; another thousand were taken prisoner.[12] It was, ironically, "the only battle that Charles ever lost or Cumberland won."[13]

The aftermath of Culloden was appalling. For three months Cumberland remained in Scotland, extirpating Jacobitism. It must be remembered that England had felt seriously threatened, that the 'Forty-five was only one of several attempts to reinstate the Stuarts, and that many of the soldiers who committed the outrages were Scots themselves; but whatever allowances are made, the fact remains that the insensitive, thick-headed, arrogant young Duke left behind him a record of brutality and vindictiveness that has few equals and that won him the sobriquet of "Butcher Cumberland." The countryside was laid waste; mansions, farms, crofts burned; men, women and children dragged out and murdered, often hanged or bayonetted beside their blazing barns, without regard whether they had actually been involved in the uprising or not. Droves of cattle were driven away to the Lowlands or to England.[14] The two Skye chiefs, Norman MacLeod and Sir Alexander MacDonald of Sleat, marched the length of Glenmoriston destroying everything, including tools, ploughs, harrows and stone querns for grinding meal.[15]

When Lord President Forbes remonstrated with the Duke, urging him to proceed in accordance with the laws of the country, Cumberland exclaimed, "The laws of the country, my lord! I'll make a brigade give laws, by God." And he said contemptuously to an officer: "That old woman [Forbes] talked to me about humanity."[16]

The hunt for the defeated Prince was on at once. He did not, as he had promised to do, stand his ground so long as he had a man remaining with him, or, if he could not conquer, die. He ran.

With Cumberland's men on his heels, he slipped from house to house through the Great Glen, endangering the life of each of his hosts in turn, until after ten days he came back to Arisaig where he had started nine months earlier. From there in the twilight he went aboard an eight-oared boat with four friends and eight boatmen and set out through a night of storm for the isles. His friends were Captain John William O'Sullivan, who had been one of the Seven Men of Moidart, a forty-six-year-old Irishman who had served with distinction in the French army and had been the adjutant and quartermaster general and — many Scotsmen felt — the evil genius of Charles's army; Colonel Felix O'Neil, a former officer of a famous Franco-Irish regiment, who had come from Paris to join Charles shortly before Culloden; Father Allan MacDonald, a native of the isles and one of Clanranald's men, who acted as Charles's chaplain and confessor; and Donald MacLeod of Galtergill in Skye, the steersman of the boat, an old man whose wife was a cousin of Flora's.

For the next two months Charles "skulked" in the outer

Hebrides, waiting and hoping for a French ship to come and take him away, while Cumberland directed the search for him from Fort Augustus. Commanding the Duke of Argyll's troops and the independent companies of MacLeods and MacDonalds was Major General John Campbell of Mamore. The captain of one of the MacDonald companies was Hugh of Armadale; of another, Allan MacDonald, whom Flora was later to marry. Under Campbell also was Captain Caroline Scott, a Lowlander in the regular army, well known for his cruelty. Commodore Thomas Smith of the 40-gun battleship *Eltham,* a sensible and humane man, was in command of the King's navy in the western waters, but under him Captain John Ferguson of the *Furnace* sloop of war, an Aberdonian, was notorious for his brutality and was, according to Mac-Donald of Baleshare, "the most bent of any" to capture the Prince.[17] Other ships that scoured the Minch and the Sea of the Hebrides watching the lochs and shores of the islands like cats at mouseholes were the *Terror,* the *Fury,* the *Baltimore,* the *Raven,* the *Trident,* the *Triton,* the *Happy Janet.* Commodore Smith and Captain Charles Knowles of the *Bridgewater* (24 guns) intercepted various small French vessels sent to pick up fugitives from the Highland army, but two large French privateers eluded them.[18]

The young fugitive for whom this wide and strangling net was spread crept from hiding place to hiding place, on foot or by boat, weather-worn, dressed in shabby tartan, often cold and hungry but seldom thirsty, usually dirty, plagued with diarrhoea but determinedly cheerful. "Very canty and jocose" were the words that MacDonald of Baleshare used about him.[19] "He won more hearts in his distress," says Andrew Lang, "than in his hour of triumph. His conduct in the heather was brave, enduring, gay, considerate and contented. He was born to love the open air and to take pleasure in the severest physical fatigues."[20]

Though it was well known to the people of the islands

who he was and where he was, and though thirty thousand pounds represented unimaginable riches, no one betrayed him, even among those who had opposed him. This is a proud record for any people. Donald MacLeod of Galtergill, the faithful old helmsman, when captured and questioned, spoke for them all: "Thirty thousand pounds! Though I had gotten't I could not have enjoyed it eight and forty hours. Conscience would have gotten up on me. That money could not have kept it down. And tho' I could have gotten all England and Scotland for my pains I would not have allowed a hair of his body to be touch'd if I could help it." To which General Campbell replied, "I will not say that you are in the wrong."[21]

When Charles was for a short time at Rossinish, the easternmost point of Benbecula, old Clanranald, who had stood out against the rising, called on him to pay his respects and to take him food and drink. At this time Flora Mac-Donald had come from Skye to visit her brother at Milton, and soon after she got there she went to Nunton to see the Clanranalds. While she was there, Colonel O'Neil came from the Prince to Nunton to learn what he could of troop movements, and he met Flora for the first time. In 1789 she wrote an account of their meeting to Sir John MacPherson, which was couched in the third person.

Miss Flora MacDonald was on a visit to her brother in South Uist in 1746 when Prince Charles came to that country back from the Lews [Lewis] and Harris after being Disappointed of a vessel to carry him abroad. Collonel O'Neil who was then along with the prince met her at Clan Ranald's house and introducing a conversation with her about him ask'd her what she would give for a sight of the Prince. She reply'd that as she had not had that happyness before, she did not look for it now, but that a sight of him would make her happy, tho' he was on a hill and she on another. Nothing further pass'd at that time.[22]

But O'Neil had seen Flora and made up his mind about her.

The most comfortable part of the Prince's eight weeks in the Long Island was the three weeks he spent in a forester's hut in Glen Corradale in South Uist. Glen Corradale was a valley on the eastern side of the island, not more than seven miles from Milton, between the mountains of Hecla and Ben More. From a cave in the hill above the hut he could look down on the Minch and see the vessels on the prowl for him there. With him there were three or four MacDonalds who were officers in young Clanranald's regiment and some stout fellows as guards, and the three who had been with him ever since he left Borrodale, Father Allan MacDonald, O'Neil and O'Sullivan. To them old Clanranald had added a young man of the Prince's own age, Neil MacEachain MacDonald, who was to take an important, if brief, part in his story.

Neil MacEachain MacDonald belonged to a branch of the Clanralds who were tacksmen at Howbeg in South Uist. He had been educated for the priesthood at the Scots College at Douai under the patronage of Aeneas MacDonald the banker, but giving up the idea of taking orders had returned to the islands and acted as tutor for Clanranald's sons. When young Clanranald was sent to France to be educated, Neil went with him as his tutor. Both had returned to Benbecula shortly before Charles arrived in Scotland. Neil spoke French well, and this was probably one reason why Clanranald sent him to the Prince, in case they might want to talk together without being understood by those around them. The gentle and studious Neil was considered by other MacDonalds "very timorous,"[23] and it was implied that this was why he was not an officer in Clanranald's regiment. Actually Clanranald's regiment was made up of clansmen from the mainland, not the islands, and Neil's conduct was not in the least timorous during the time of testing that was to follow.

While the Prince and his companions were at Glen
Corradale, they enjoyed hunting the muirfowl with which
the country abounded. They were visited by the gentlemen
of the countryside, who brought gifts, usually bottles of
brandy. Clanranald came, and Boisdale, his half brother;
Hugh MacDonald of Baleshare, a small island off North
Uist, came and spent three days and nights. Baleshare
brought with him not only brandy but a gift from Lady
Margaret MacDonald of gazettes, a purse of fifty guineas
and a letter telling of the movements of the independent
companies. Fifty English shillings would have been more
use to him, Charles commented wryly; changing a guinea
was not easy in the islands and much too conspicuous. Neil
MacEachain said of the Prince, "He took care to warm his
stomach every morning with a hearty bumper of brandy, of
which he always drank a vast deal, for he was seen to drink a
whole bottle of a day without being in the least concerned."[24]

Both Colonel O'Neil and Neil MacEachain told of going
on long walks through the hills to find out the whereabouts
of the troops, and O'Neil in those walks came sometimes to
Milton and talked with Flora and her brother. He learned
their history, that their mother lived in Skye and that their
stepfather was Hugh of Armadale.

The determination of General Campbell to smoke
Charles out by landing troops in the north and in the south
of the Long Island and having them march toward the
middle broke up the time of respite at Glen Corradale and
set the Prince on the run again. The crisis came when with
his little band he approached Loch Boisdale, hoping for
help, only to learn that MacDonald of Boisdale had been
taken prisoner the day before and carried to the *Furnace*
and that Captain Caroline Scott with his regulars was but a
mile away.

When things were at this pass, Hugh MacDonald of
Armadale, then in Benbecula with his company, sent word

to Charles that his situation was now impossible and that if the Prince would take his (Hugh's) advice, he would get him to Skye to the protection of Lady Margaret MacDonald.[25] That Armadale, a captain on the government side, was risking a charge of treason is obvious. That he might be setting a trap did not occur to any of them — and of course he was not. "Honest Hugh" was faithful to the demands of compassion. "It is not so easy," said Edinburgh University's famous Professor John Stuart Blackie, "to be heroic on the cool water of human brotherhood as on the hot wine of political enthusiasm."[26]

The little band of hunted men decided to separate and let each man shift for himself. They left O'Sullivan under a rock with most of the Prince's baggage. Father Allan took to the hills and was soon captured and consigned to the *Furnace*. Charles, with MacEachain and O'Neil, set out across the hills toward Milton.

On the night of June 20, which was full moonlight, they sought out Flora MacDonald and asked her help. The ten days that followed made Flora Scotland's most loved heroine.

✿ 3 ✿

Flora to the Rescue

FIVE people told the story of those ten days, or parts of them, in considerable detail: Flora herself, Colonel Felix O'Neil, Neil MacEachain MacDonald, Donald Roy Mac-Donald and Malcolm MacLeod. Flora's story is told three times: first when she was being questioned by General Campbell after her capture; a second time when she talked with Dr. Burton of York, who took down her statement for posterity; and finally in 1789, when at the request of Sir John MacPherson, her friend and perhaps her cousin, she wrote an account of those days as seen from a perspective of forty-four years. Neil MacEachain's story, which was not signed but which was known to be his through internal evidence, had a curious history. The manuscript turned up nearly a hundred years later in the possession of a hairdresser in Paris, who had acquired it when MacEachain's papers were scattered during the French Revolution;[1] it was published in the *New Monthly Magazine* in 1840 and reprinted in *The Origins of the 'Forty-five* by Dr. Blaikie. Colonel O'Neil wrote a Journal, which he sent to the Countess of Dundonald in 1747 and which was preserved in *The Lyon in Mourning*, the collection of firsthand accounts of the 'Forty-five painstakingly gathered by Bishop Forbes immediately after the uprising. Malcolm MacLeod and Donald Roy Mac-Donald, who were involved only in the ninth and tenth days, wrote their accounts at the request of Bishop Forbes.

There are occasional discrepancies among the several narratives but only slight ones; far more often they confirm

45

and supplement each other, one adding a detail which another omitted. Some of the apparent discrepancies can be explained by the jealousy that developed between Colonel O'Neil and Neil MacEachain. Neither mentioned the other if he could possibly avoid it, and each wrote with a slight but distinct slant in favor of himself. Donald MacLeod of Galtergill felt that O'Neil claimed entirely too much for himself. "Faith," said Donald to Bishop Forbes, "he taks ower mickell to himself and he is not blate to mind himsell sae mickell and to forget others that behooved to do much more than he could do in sic a case."[2] Blaikie, author of the invaluable *Itinerary of Prince Charles*, makes use of all these accounts in plotting the Prince's course during this period, so that we can follow in detail almost from hour to hour the happenings of those memorable ten days.

The twentieth of June fell on a Friday that year. The moon was full. A midsummer night in the Hebrides is scarcely dark at all, but that moonlight night must have been bright enough for every feature and facial expression to show clearly when those four young people met and talked: Colonel Felix O'Neil, the Irish soldier of fortune born in Rome, who had served in France and Spain before he came to Scotland; Neil MacEachain MacDonald, the studious, the gentle, the musical (he played the violin); the Prince in his shabby kilt, lean and freckled but undeniably royal; and Flora, slight and short, "well-shaped," with wide dark eyes and the dazzlingly fair skin and bright color of the island girls.

It was the custom in the Hebrides as in the Scandinavian countries for the girls of a family to take the cattle up into the hill pastures in the summer months. Flora, visiting her brother Angus, went with the cows up on to Sheaval, the 750-foot hill behind Milton. At night she slept in the shieling called Alisary, a small low building no more than a shelter.

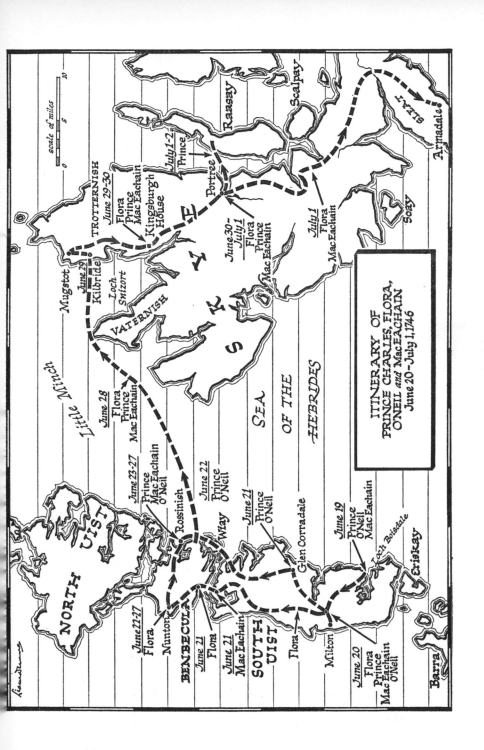

ITINERARY OF PRINCE CHARLES, FLORA, O'NEIL and MacEACHAIN
June 20 – July 1, 1746

She was asleep there when the three fugitives drew near in the moonlight. She wrote in her account of 1789:

The colonel some time after came to her at a shieling of her brother's where she then stayed and being about midnight sent in a cousin of her own who had been a long time with him and the Prince to awake her, which he did and told her that they were both without and wanted instantly to speak with her. She was surprised and wanted to know what they had to say to her but went out as fast as she could throw on some of her cloaths and met the collonel at the door, leaving the prince behind the hutt.[3]

This is the only indication there is that Neil MacEachain MacDonald of Howbeg was related to Flora. It has been questioned whether the MacEachains of Howbeg were Mac-Donalds at all but might have been MacLeans instead.[4] As Neil later dropped the name MacEachain altogether, using only the MacDonald, and as Flora here claims him for cousin, it seems probable — if not very important — that he was indeed of the Clanranald branch of the clan.

Colonel O'Neil in his account omits MacEachain altogether and declares that it was he who first approached Flora.

I quitted the Prince at some distance from the hut and went myself with the design of being informed if the independent companies were to pass that way next day as we had been informed. The young lady answered in the negative saying they would not pass till the day after. I then told her I had brought a friend to see her. She with some emotion asked if it was the Prince.[5]

MacEachain for his part omits the Colonel, saying merely that he himself left the Prince a little way off and went into the shieling and awakened Flora. According to him, it was the Prince himself who proposed the plan for his escape, but O'Neil and Flora herself agree that it was O'Neil.

"He immediately," wrote Flora in 1789, "proposed to her (as he knew she had a desire to come to Sleat in Sky where her mother then lived and did not like to stay longer in Uist, as all there were in confusion) to take the prince along with her as her servant dressed in woman's clothes."

He himself explained that he pointed out to her that "this seemed the more feasible as the young lady's father being captain of an independent company could afford a pass for herself and servant to go visit her mother."[6]

The plan presumably had originated with Hugh of Armadale. Why, since he was in communication with the family at Milton, who knew about the troop movements, he had not himself sent some word of it to Flora is not clear. Possibly he thought that the Prince would be more persuasive than he would himself, or perhaps he had on an impulse sent his message to the Prince and waited for Charles to pick it up and act on it. At all events, it was a new idea to Flora and not a welcome one. Though MacEachain insisted that she "joyfully agreed,"[7] this was not the case. Objections came crowding to her mind.

O'Neil says that she answered

with the greatest respect and loyalty but declined, saying Sir Alexander MacDonald was too much her friend (for her) to be the instrument of his ruine. I endeavoured to obviate this by assuring her that Sir Alexander was not in the country and that she could with the greatest facility convey the Prince to her mother's house as she lived close by the water side.[8]

Sir Alexander was at that time in Fort Augustus with Cumberland — probably the reason why his wife Lady Margaret felt free to send newspapers and money to Baleshare for the Prince.

O'Neil reported another scruple of Flora's, that she feared the tongues of the unkind and suspicious. "You need not fear your character [reputation]," he assured her, "for by this you will gain yourself an immortal character. But if you will still entertain fears about your character I shall (by an oath) marry you directly if you please."[9]

This kind offer no one seems to have taken seriously — perhaps it was made only in phantasy afterwards — but it is interesting in view of MacEachain's later assertion that O'Neil had fallen in love with Flora.

O'Neil went on to urge upon her "the honor and immortality that would redound to her by such a glorious action," and after the Prince himself had added his word, telling her "the sense he would always retain of so conspicuous a service," she at length acquiesced.[10]

Flora herself did not record these answers to what she called her "many qualms and objections." Perhaps after forty-three years she did not remember them. Her reasons both for declining and for yielding were more direct and feminine.

She told him as there were so many dangers to encounter it would grieve her more that he [Charles] should be taken along with her than in any other way, and begg'd that he would not insist on her undertaking that piece of service. He answer'd that there was no other method to extricate him out of his present danger and that tho' she denied him [O'Neil] he was sure she would not deny him [Charles] as soon as she saw him.

"Don't think sir," said she, "that I am quite so fainthearted as that comes to."

He then whistled, the prince appeared, he introduced him to Miss MacDonald and spoke to him in Italian, telling him her scruples and that she deny'd him her undertaking the propos'd scheme.[11]

They stood now, the four of them, on the hillside with the cattle around them and the moon shining on the Atlantic in the distance below.

The prince himself then spoke to her, being previously well known to the situation of the country, and told her she would be quite safe in undertaking what he wanted, as her step-father, Hugh MacDonald of Armdale, was commanding officer there, a gentleman he knew himself and waited on him personally when he landed first on the mainland and was sure he wished him well, and that he would give her a pass to Sky.

She still insisted on the danger, but her former resolution failed her and [she] undertook the voyage provided she got her step-father's pass.

They took, she went on to say, " a little refreshment." MacEachain told what it was. "She brought to him [Charles] a part of the best cheer she had; among the rest was a large bowl of cream, of which he took two or three hearty go-downs and his fellow-travellers swallowed the rest." (The *s* in "fellow-travellers" is MacEachain's only acknowledgement of O'Neil's presence at this crucial interview.) She also gave them bread and cheese to take with them.

After they had fixed on the point of Rossinish on the east coast of Benbecula for their meeting place, the Prince and his two companions went on over the hills toward Glen Corradale, and Flora was left alone in the shieling with the realization of what she had undertaken.

She must have told her brother the next day what she had promised, for we find him and his wife Penelope later on the scene. After sending a message to the Prince, Flora set out that day for Nunton, evidently with the idea of enlisting Clanranald's help and expecting to encounter her stepfather somewhere along the way.

When she came to the ford between South Uist and Benbecula, she was stopped on the Benbecula side by soldiers who asked for her passport. She demanded spiritedly to know to whom they belonged, and when she was told that the captain was Hugh MacDonald of Armadale she refused to answer any further questions till she saw the captain himself. He was evidently not there at the time, for she was held prisoner overnight.[12]

Meanwhile, Charles with O'Neil and MacEachain came
at sunrise to a place about three miles from Glen Corradale.
There they spent the day in the heather, without any food
except the bread and cheese that Flora had given them.
About four o'clock Flora's messenger arrived to tell them
that all was well, and they were all for joining her at once.
The messenger qualified his first statement with the news
that the fords were guarded and they could not get through.
Here was a dilemma. A "man of the country" promised them
a boat next day, and the Prince that night at eight sent
MacEachain, who knew the country well, to scout out the
ground and get what news he could, telling him to be sure to
be back by four the next afternoon.

MacEachain set out, found the ford guarded as they had
been told, was in his turn arrested and was held overnight on
the South Uist side of the ford.

At low tide the next morning, Sunday the twenty-second
of June, MacEachain was escorted across to Benbecula and
taken to the captain. When he went in he found Flora
comfortably having breakfast with her stepfather.

He took her aside and asked if everything was ready. She
replied that she had not got to Lady Clanranald yet but that
she was going within half an hour to consult with her. She
continued confidently that she and "Lady Clan" would go
together that afternoon to Rossinish with clothes and provisions and urged MacEachain to return to the Prince and get
him to Rossinish as fast as he could.[13]

Flora had had a satisfactory talk with her stepfather.
"She told him what she had undertaken, what the prince
said of himself [i.e., of Armadale] and that he knew him,
which Mr. MacDonald acknowledged."[14] They were evidently both sure of Lady Clanranald's help.

Armadale then gave his stepdaughter the necessary
passes, for herself, a manservant and a woman, Betty Burke.
It was Armadale's idea that Flora should not go on this

enterprise unattended, and he had settled on MacEachain, the trusted member of the Clanranald household and possibly a cousin, as protector, not so much for the Prince as for Flora. With the passes Armdale gave Flora a letter to his wife to show anyone who questioned her. The original letter was destroyed after Flora was taken prisoner to keep it from falling into the hands of the military, but those who had seen it remembered every word of it. Flora, when shown a copy of it in 1748, made some minor corrections and approved it.

My Dear Marion, I have sent your daughter from this country, lest she should be in any way frightened with the troops lying here. She has got one Betty Burke, an Irish girl, who, as she tells me, is a good spinster. If her spinning please you, you can keep her till she spin all your lint, or if you have any wool to spin, you may employ her. I have sent Neil MacEachainn along with your daughter and Betty Burke to take care of them.

I am,

Your dutiful husband,

Hugh MacDonald

Fortified with the passes, the letter and Hugh's approval, Flora went on to Nunton and told her story to Lady Clan and doubtless to Clanranald himself, who appears to have been there, though he took no overt part in the affair.

Their first setback was that there were no women's clothes in the house big enough to fit the Prince, and the whole household had to turn to and make an outfit. In the days before sewing machines this was no small undertaking. "The ladies were busy night and day," wrote MacEachain, "getting a dress made for the Prince and other things."

Flora stayed at Nunton from Sunday the twenty-second of June till Friday the twenty-seventh, while the Prince hid under rocks near Rossinish in the rain and fumed. The delay was due partly to the business of making the clothes and partly to consideration of an alternative plan, suggested possibly by Clanranald. Instead of sending the Prince off precariously with Flora, why not put him under the care of a man, of, indeed, MacDonald of Baleshare, who had already been so active and helpful, visiting the Prince at Glen Corradale with his gifts?

We owe the story of these days of delay and uncertainty to MacEachain and O'Neil.

On Sunday afternoon MacEachain had returned from the ford to find the Prince and O'Neil waiting where he had left them. He had got hold of a small boat, and that night he rowed them across Benbecula Bay at its widest point, well away from the ford, to the island of Wiay, where they spent the night.

The next day, Monday, they set out in the pouring rain, landed on Benbecula and tramped across the moors to Ross-inish. Benbecula, about seven miles square, was the flattest of the islands, with only one hill, Rueval, in the center of it and that no more than 400 feet high. It was a day, wrote MacEachain, of "vehement wind," and anyone who has been in the Hebrides during one of those sudden gales for which they are famous knows how vehement the wind can be. Drenched and shivering, they reached the hut of one of Clanranald's tenants near Rossinish and were taken aback not to find Flora waiting for them there. They told the farmer and his wife that they were Irish refugees and were taken in for the night.

Early the next morning, Tuesday, the farmer's wife woke them to warn them that the militia were in the habit of coming there to buy milk and that they had better leave. So out they turned into the rain and went to huddle under a rock near the shore. The Prince met wind and rain and cold with "incomparable patience," but the swarms of midges that day wrung from him "hideous cries and complaints."

He wanted to send MacEachain right off to Nunton to

54

tell Flora to hurry, but MacEachain was unwilling to leave him with O'Neil, who did not know the country. Accordingly O'Neil was deputed to make the expedition, with a guide. He was, said MacEachain sourly, "mightily well pleased to be entrusted with that embassy, not so much to further the prince's affairs as to be in company with Miss Flora, for whom he professed a great kindness at that time."

Later in the day, after the militia had left, Charles and MacEachain returned to the farmhouse and drank frothed milk. That night, wrapped in his wet plaid, Charles slept on "the leaf of a door covered with an old ragged sail." O'Neil spent the night comfortably at Nunton, where Flora told him the plan for sending the Prince to Baleshare instead of taking him across to Skye.

He and MacEachain give conflicting accounts of what happened on Thursday.

O'Neil recorded that he had immediately despatched a boy to the Prince with the news that he was to stay with a cousin of Flora's in North Uist and he appointed a place to meet, "whither his royal highness came." Baleshare, however, refused to receive them,

alleging for a motive he was a vassal to Sir Alexander MacDonald. In this unexpected exigence being a small half-mile of a captain and fifty men, we hastened for Rushness [Rossinish] being apprized the enemy had just abandoned it. The Prince sent me to acquaint Miss Flora of our disappointment and to entreat her to keep her promise as there was no time to be lost. She faithfully promised next day. I remained with her that night, the Prince remaining at Rushness attended by a little herd-boy.

It is not clear whether O'Neil is here reducing MacEachain to the status of a herdboy or whether the herdboy was the messenger who went back and forth and who possibly stayed that night at Rossinish so as to be on hand

55

for further errands. MacEachain's story in any case is different.

According to him the guide who went with O'Neil to Nunton returned with a roasted fowl, a couple of bottles of wine and a letter from O'Neil, which MacEachain did not see but which he thought was an apology for O'Neil's not coming himself. He did not mention the Baleshare plan at all and possibly was not told of it.

Flora herself says only that "another scheme was proposed, that the Prince should go under the care of a gentleman to the northward but that failed and they returned to the original plan." She said also that O'Neil went back and forth frequently between Nunton and the Prince, "to inform her where he was, what steps had been taken for her voyage and at the same time to hasten her to get her affairs in Readiness for going off."[15]

All accounts of what happened on Friday the twenty-seventh are substantially the same. In the morning the Prince and MacEachain returned to Rueval, the 400-foot hill where they skulked in the daytime; to which in the course of the day two men came to tell them that the boat for Skye was ready. The two men the Prince already knew, for they had rowed in the boat that had brought him to Benbecula from the mainland two months earlier. They were brothers, John and Roderick MacDonald of South Uist, cousins of Flora's, both lieutenants in young Clanranald's regiment. MacEachain then left the Prince on Rueval with the two MacDonalds and hurried off to Nunton, where he evidently took some satisfaction in sending O'Neil back to the Prince.

The people at Nunton were now ready. A large party of them, Lady Clanranald, her daughter Peggy, aged seven, Flora, her brother Milton and his wife, set out by another road than the one O'Neil had taken, so that they could get a boat to Rossinish. When they arrived there, the Prince and O'Neil, who had got there first, were on the shore to greet them. The Prince handed Lady Clanranald to the cottage while O'Neil escorted Flora. When the supper of roasted liver, heart and kidneys of a bullock was ready — Flora said the Prince himself helped to prepare it — they all sat down, "very hearty and merry," Lady Clanranald on the Prince's left, Flora as his protectress in the place of honor on his right. It would be interesting to know what that small girl Peggy thought of it all — the farmer's dim, windowless, smoky room, the rainy gray twilight beyond the open door, the merriment sharpened by danger; the young prince, handsome in spite of his freckles and his midge bites, wrapped in his royalty as securely as in his shabby plaid — or old Clanranald, sitting at home, hearing the sound of marching men draw near.

In the midst of the supper at Rossinish there came a herdboy from Clanranald, perhaps the same one who had been running back and forth these two days, with the news that General Campbell was landing his men within three miles of them. They jumped up in consternation and confusion. Each one carrying whatever came to his hand, they ran to the boat and crossed Loch Uskevaugh, a sea loch to the north, and landed on the other side, where they finished their supper.

By this time morning had come. At eight there was another message from Nunton. Captain Ferguson had slept in Lady Clanranald's bed that night, and General Campbell and a party of men were at the house and wanted her there by twelve or the house would suffer. She and her daughter went off forthwith.

When they reached Nunton, Lady Clanranald was "strictly examined" by General Campbell, who wanted to know where she had been. She replied that she had gone to visit a sick child at some distance, whereupon he demanded to know the child's name and where it lived but was unable to shake her story. Skeptical but baffled, the soldiers withdrew from Nunton, to return several days later.[16]

After Lady Clan and Peggy had gone, the rest of the group, sobered, began to break up. The question arose at once: what was to be done about Colonel O'Neil? Was he to go with Charles and Flora — and MacEachain — or to stay behind? He insisted that he must accompany the Prince. Flora, displaying unexpected firmness, said no and stuck to it in the face of the earnest pleas of both the Prince and O'Neil. He was not mentioned in the passport; he did not speak the language of the country; he was a stranger and would arouse suspicion in anyone who saw him. According to O'Neil, the Prince declared that he would not go if O'Neil were not of the party, and Flora countered that she would give the whole thing up if he were. Flora said only, "Miss MacDonald would by no means consent to his going along and the Prince himself seemed willing he should go but did not insist much with Miss MacDonald." So O'Neil was left behind. He conceded later that it was a wise decision. He went off with Milton and his wife toward South Uist, where he found O'Sullivan and joined him.

Milton took with him also Charles's pistols. The Prince had intended to carry them himself under his spinster's dress, but this idea too Flora vetoed.

"If any person should happen to search them," she said, "the pistols would only serve to make a discovery."

To which the Prince rejoined, "Indeed, Miss, if we happen to meet with any that will go that narrowly to work in searching as what you mean they will certainly discover me at any rate."[17]

But she would not yield, and Milton took the pistols for safekeeping. The Prince was left with a "short, heavy cudgel, with which he designed to do his best to knock down any single person that should attack him."

Flora was remarkably ready with swift and firm decisions; she knew just what she was willing to do and could withstand the persuasions of both those persuasive men, the handsome Prince and that attractive Irish colonel. Looking between the lines, one sees some protective man briefing her beforehand, either old Clanranald or her brother Milton.

When they were alone the Prince got into his costume, a printed linen gown of a white background sprigged with blue, a light-colored quilted petticoat, a cap and apron and a hooded cloak of dun camlet "made after the Irish fashion," shoes, stockings and a pair of blue garters. "The company being gone," MacEachain wrote, "the Prince stript of his own cloaths, was dressed by Miss Flora in his new attire, but he could not keep his hands from adjusting his head dress, which he cursed a thousand times."

It was still too early to set out. Wet and tired, they made a fire on a rock to keep themselves warm while the slow hours dragged on. They had one fright. A cutter and four wherries filled with armed men came past, apparently making for the shore. Hastily they put out the fire and scrambled to hide in the heather, but the boats full of General Campbell's men went on without stopping.[18]

By eight o'clock the skies had cleared and night had come — or what passed for night in the Hebrides. The boat came out from its hiding place, and they embarked.

4

Over the Sea to Skye

THE boat was a shallop of nine cubits, an open boat about eighteen feet long with a mast and oars. There were five boatmen, four to row and one at the helm. All were from the Long Island and two were cousins of Flora MacDonald's. They knew, of course, who Betty Burke was and that they were risking their lives in the adventure; they were also aware that they were forgoing a chance at thirty thousand pounds.

The night was clear and calm when they started out,[1] and the Prince in his sprigged dress and fancy cap was in high spirits. He shared the milk that Lady Clanranald had provided for the voyage, drinking out of the bottle "Jock-fellow-like" with the boatmen, and he decreed that the half bottle of wine, all that was left of Lady Clanranald's store after many visits from bands of the military, should be saved for Flora "lest she should faint with the cold and other inconveniences of a night passage."[2]

About midnight a gale came up from the west, with a thick mist and heavy rain that blotted out all sight of land. The boatmen, who had no compass, were not sure of their course.[3] Flora became very much alarmed, and the Prince sang Jacobite songs to her until she fell asleep — "The King Shall Enjoy His Own Again" and "The Twenty-ninth of May," songs of the 'Fifteen which he may have learned as a child from his father.[4] Later on some small bustle in the boat woke her, and she found the Prince spreading his hands over her to keep a boatman from stumbling over her in the dark.[5]

60

By morning the rain had stopped and the wind veered around to the north, blowing so hard in their teeth that for an hour and a half they could not tell whether they made any way or not.[6] Charles, still cheerful after a sleepless night, offered to relieve the most tired of the boatmen but his offer was not accepted. They came at length to the point of Vaternish, Skye's western wing, where they would have landed, but they found soldiers posted there to watch for boats from the Long Island.

"They were so near the shore," wrote Flora,

that they saw the men armed, but luckily it was low water and the shore so rough that they wou'd not launch out their boat. They then saw some of the men running up to the house where their commanding officer lay, they suppos'd to inform him about the boat. Miss MacDonald said she was afraid they would now be taken. Don't be afraid Miss said the prince, we will not be taken yet. You see it is low water and before they can launch their boats out over that rough shore we will get in below those high rocks and they will lose sight of us, which they did.[7]

They put into the "clift of a rock" or a seacave, where they rested and ate the bread and butter provided by Lady Clanranald. The milk having been drunk during the night, they washed the bread down with water that trickled over the rock. Setting out once more they rowed about twelve miles across Loch Snizort to a place called Kilbride, in Trotternish, where they landed "within a cannon-shot" of Sir Alexander MacDonald's house.

Duntulm Castle, about five miles to the north, was the original stronghold of the MacDonalds of Sleat, but for some reason — some say because of the death of a child who fell from the ramparts into the sea — Sir Alexander's father had abandoned it fifteen years earlier and built the much more modest house that Sir Alexander and Lady Margaret with their three small children, James, Susan and Alexander, now occupied. It stood on Lake Columkille (since drained) on the site of an ancient monastery, from which probably came its name, Monkstadt, corrupted to Mugstot.

Flora and MacEachain left the Prince in the boat on the shore while they went up to the house to seek Lady Margaret's help. Before they went they primed the boatmen with a story in case any soldiers should discover them: they were to say that the Prince was Miss MacDonald's maid and they were to "curse her for a lazy jade, what was she good for since she did not attend her mistress."[8]

As the two approached the house, they met a servant of Lady Margaret's, from whom they learned that there were guests at Mugstot that day, Mrs. John MacDonald of Kirkibost, Alexander MacDonald of Kingsburgh, who was chief factor for the chief, Sir Alexander MacDonald of Sleat, and Lieutenant MacLeod of the Skye militia, with four of his men. The rest of his command was in the neighborhood hunting for the Prince. They must have looked at each other in consternation.

Flora sent the maid ahead to tell Lady Margaret that Miss MacDonald had stopped in to see her on her way home from South Uist, and in a few minutes the woman returned to lead Flora to a room where she found Lady Margaret alone.

Lady Margaret already knew something of what was up. Mrs. MacDonald of Kirkibost had come the day before to tell her that the Prince was on his way to Skye. Though Mrs. MacDonald's husband was captain of one of the independent companies, she had been stopped by soldiers on the way from North Uist and to her indignation strictly examined. When Flora appeared, Lady Margaret was thrown into a panic. It was one thing to send newspapers and money to the Prince and get graceful little notes in return; it was quite another to have him land on her beach — and the soldiers in the house.

Earlier that day, after she had got the news from Mrs.

MacDonald, she had sent a message to Donald Roy Mac-Donald, who was in the neighborhood, begging him to come to her aid. Now another person to take part in Charles's escape, and to contribute his story, appears in the record. Donald Roy MacDonald was a brother of Hugh MacDonald of Baleshare. Donald Roy, who was one of the only two of Sir Alexander's following to go out for the Prince, had been a captain in Clanranald's regiment. Wounded in the foot at Culloden, he had escaped and got to Skye to the home of Dr. John MacLean, surgeon and neighbor to Sir Alexander, where he was kept for treatment. On June twenty-second his brother Baleshare had sent a boat to him with a letter, in which was enclosed a note to Lady Margaret MacDonald in the Prince's handwriting. The letter to Lady Margaret was chiefly compliments and thanks for the gazettes and money which she had sent. Baleshare's letter to Donald Roy, however, informed him that the Prince intended to leave the Long Island and land on a small island called Fladdachuain, off Trotternish, Skye's eastern wing. Donald Roy was asked to meet the Prince there and take him necessities, especially shirts and newspapers.

Donald Roy had taken the Prince's letter to Lady Margaret, advising her to burn it, but she said that she would keep it "for the sake of him who writ it." She promptly had six of Sir Alexander's best shirts laundered for the Prince and gave Donald Roy twenty more guineas to take to him. Donald Roy went to Fladdachuain, but not finding the Prince there he had returned the money and shirts to Lady Margaret and had gone back to Dr. MacLean's house nearby.

Kingsburgh also was at Mugstot that day, but up to now Lady Margaret had not taken him into her confidence. Alexander MacDonald of Kingsburgh, a man of fifty-seven, bluff, honest, loyal, able, was her husband's factor and chief tacksman; his son Allan was lieutenant of one of Sir Alexander's independent companies. Now that the Prince had actually put himself into her hands, Lady Margaret turned to Kingsburgh. Sending Flora into the dining room to cope with Lieutenant MacLeod, she drew Kingsburgh into the garden to ask him what on earth they should do. Just as they got there Donald Roy came riding up on the doctor's horse and dismounted.

"Oh, Donald Roy," cried Lady Margaret, spreading out her hands, "we are ruined forever!"[9]

Donald Roy was "a tall, sturdy man about six foot high, exceedingly well shaped and about forty years of age." He had not been to a university but he was well educated, having studied under Mr. John MacPherson, a well-known schoolmaster in Skye, and he wrote Latin verse for his own amusement. He had turned in his weapons after Culloden to his old friend, Lieutenant MacLeod, the very man who was now in the dining room with Flora, asking her pointed questions — but not his best weapons, which he hid.

Without hesitation Kingsburgh undertook responsibility for getting the Prince safely away. It was obvious that Charles could not be harbored at Mugstot. Indeed, as Kingsburgh was quick to point out, there were too many soldiers in Skye for him to remain on the island at all; he must be passed on to the MacKenzies in the Seaforth country. He suggested that the Prince be sent by boat around the north of Trotternish to Raasay, a small island off the east coast of Skye, from which the laird, MacLeod of Raasay, could watch his opportunity to pass him on to Seaforth.

Lady Margaret objected to this plan; there was, she said, a party of soldiers posted on the shore near Duntulm who would surely see the boat as it passed. Donald Roy then suggested sending Charles overland to Portree and from there to Raasay. Unlike MacLeod of MacLeod, MacLeod of Raasay, who was head of the Lewis branch of the clan, had been out in the 'Forty-five. They were confident that he could be depended upon to help in this crisis, but Donald

Charles Edward Stuart, The Young Prince

PORTRAIT BY MAURICE DE LA TOUR

Anne MacDonald

Allan MacDonald

Roy must go first, said Kingsburgh, to make sure that the laird was willing. He himself would put the Prince on the way to Portree.

This decision made, they sent MacEachain, who had apparently been standing by disregarded during this conference, to the Prince to take him away from the shore to a safer place and to tell him that Kingsburgh would come for him in due course. They made up a bundle for the Prince to carry as if it were his mistress's baggage, but his Royal Highness, who had submitted to so many indignities, balked at this one; he disdainfully tossed the bundle away, declaring that MacEachain should carry it himself or leave it, whichever he wished.

Flora all this time was in the dining room keeping Lieutenant MacLeod interested with her feminine charm. She knew nothing about Donald Roy's presence in the garden nor of the plans that were being made there. She later told Bishop Forbes that she "could not help observing Lady Margaret often going in and out as one in great anxiety, while she in the mean time endeavoured to keep up a close chit-chat with Lieutenant MacLeod who put many questions to her, which she answered as she saw fit."[10] The Lieutenant himself was apparently too much dazzled by Flora to notice anything odd about his hostess's behavior.

After Donald Roy had gone off on his errand, still riding the doctor's horse, Kingsburgh took some wine and biscuits provided by Lady Margaret and went to find the Prince. He had trouble in discovering him at first on the hill about a mile from Mugstot to which he had been led, but the sight of a flock of sheep running was enough to tell a country man where to look, and he soon saw Charles Edward sitting patiently on a rock. The original plan had been to conduct the Prince directly to Portree — "fourteen long Scots miles" — but when Kingsburgh saw him, tired, dirty and cheerful, he decided to give him one night in a bed first. Neil Mac-

Eachain, who had conceived a passionate devotion to the Prince and must have wanted very much to go with him, was left behind to tell Flora of the plans and to escort her to Kingsburgh House. The quiet and unassuming MacEachain was consistently underestimated by the other men.

Lady Margaret invited Flora to spend the night at Mugstot, but she declined, explaining to her hostess — and to the Lieutenant — that she must be on her way home because the times were troublous. That she had now delivered her royal charge into older and stronger hands and was therefore free, her duty done, to relax at Mugstot apparently never occurred to her. Late in the afternoon she set off for Kingsburgh House on a horse supplied by Lady Margaret. Mrs. MacDonald of Kirkibost rode part of the way with her; they had MacEachain and Mrs. MacDonald's maid in attendance.

Somewhere along the way they overtook Kingsburgh and Betty Burke striding along on foot. Flora was diverted to see her former maid taking long steps and lifting her skirts high as she straddled a brook. Mrs. MacDonald tried to get a glimpse of the Prince's face but he kept it turned away. Her maid commented scornfully on the impudent-looking woman with Kingsburgh and her clumsy way of dealing with her petticoats, and MacEachain, who must have been in agony, explained that the woman was an Irish girl whom they had seen as they came from the Long Island. A group of countrypeople on their way home from church was moved to indignation by the way the impudent creature walked alongside Kingsburgh and freely talked to him.[11]

It was late when Flora, having parted from Mrs. MacDonald, reached Kingsburgh House, and the mistress of Kingsburgh had already gone to bed. When the message was brought to her that Milton's daughter had come with a friend, she said, "Milton's daughter is very welcome to come here with any company she pleases to bring, but you'll give my service to her and tell her to make free with anything in the house; for I am very sleepy and cannot see her this night."[12]

But when Kingsburgh himself came in and told her who the guest was, the good lady got up in a hurry and with the help of her daughter Anne, Mrs. MacAllister, who was there on a visit, prepared a supper. During the nearly twenty-four hours that the Prince was in the house they served his meals themselves in order to keep the servants from seeing him.

After Mrs. MacDonald and her daughter and Flora had gone to bed, Kingsburgh and the Prince sat up late over a bowl of punch. And then at last Charles had a bath and was put to sleep for the first time in months in a comfortable bed with clean sheets. Neil MacEachain slept in the room with him, but unfortunately MacEachain's manuscript breaks off abruptly just after the meeting with the country people at the brook, and so we do not have his account of the night at Kingsburgh House.

In the morning Mrs. MacDonald went early to Flora to get the whole story from her. What, she asked at once, had been done with the boatmen? She was disturbed to hear that they had gone back to South Uist, after being sworn not to tell what they had done. The boat should have been sunk, Mrs. MacDonald said, and the boatmen hidden in Skye, "for once the military get hold of them they will terrify them out of their senses and make them break their oath." The portrait of Mrs. MacDonald shows a sweet, motherly, practical face under the white muslin cap. She had a shrewd knowledge of people; one of the boatmen was subsequently caught and threatened with torture, and he did confess.[13]

The exhausted Charles slept so late that morning that Flora got worried, but he woke at last. The day passed quietly. Kingsburgh had sent a message to Donald Roy at Portree to the effect that Miss MacDonald had been so tired that she had stayed all night at Kingsburgh House instead of going to Portree as she had intended, and he asked the

Captain to get her a boat to Strath because it would be easier for her to go over sea than by land.

Small incidents of the day were remembered. Mrs. MacDonald wanted a lock of the Prince's hair and got Flora to ask for it. "He complied instantly," and either Flora or Mrs. MacAllister cut it (both claimed to have done it); afterwards Mrs. MacDonald must have divided it with Flora, for there is a locket at Dunvegan Castle with the Prince's hair in it which one of Flora's granddaughters gave to one of the MacLeods. The sheets he slept in were carefully folded up and put away for Mrs. MacDonald to be buried in.

In the evening the Prince, still in his Betty Burke clothes in spite of his protests, left the house and started on the long walk across the hills to Portree, with "one trusty man and a boy" to guide him by cattle paths through the heather. It was raining again. After he had gone a little way he stopped in a bit of woods to change his clothes and put on the kilt and jacket and plaid that Kingsburgh had given him. The Betty Burke costume was hidden under a rock and later recovered by his admirers and parceled out among them.

Flora with MacEachain still in attendance went on horseback by the road and reached Portree first. The place had a name (Port of the King, for James IV, who had visited there) but it was no more than a few houses and a primitive inn on the shore of Loch Portree, across the mouth of which lay the island of Raasay. The innkeeper was a man named Charles MacNabb.

Flora went into the inn to wait and found Donald Roy there. According to MacNabb, they had supper before the rest came.[14]

Donald Roy had spent the day making arrangements. By good luck he had come on Rona, Raasay's eldest son, on Skye. Rona had told him that the laird was on the mainland in Knoydart but he agreed himself to take the Prince to Raasay. Rona, with his younger brother Murdoch and their cousin Malcolm MacLeod, was now waiting with a small boat on the shore half a mile from Portree.

When the Prince still did not come, Donald Roy restlessly went out hoping to meet him, but it was raining hard and his foot hurt, and soon he was back again. Presently a boy came to the door and asked the landlord if Donald Roy MacDonald was there. Donald Roy sent the boy to the kitchen and went out to greet the Prince, who "took him," he said, "in his arms and by way of salutation put his head over one shoulder of the Captain and then over the other." Donald Roy said he was sorry for the rain and the Prince replied, "I am more sorry that our lady should be all abused with rain." They went back into the inn, where Flora was waiting.

There was a fire on the hearth, a clean, dry shirt and food (bread, butter, cheese and roasted fish) and drink. Charles, Donald Roy and Neil MacEachain drank a bottle of whisky and the Prince bought another one, changing a guinea to pay for it. He would have liked to spend the night at the inn, but Malcolm MacLeod came to knock at the door and beg the Prince to hurry, for Rona and his brother were waiting in the rain with the boat.[15]

Malcolm MacLeod of Brea in Raasay, who now enters the story, was a man of thirty-four, a second cousin of the laird. He had been a captain in the Prince's army, had been wounded in the shoulder at Culloden but had escaped and recovered. He was a well-set-up man and something of a dandy, dressed for his adventure in scarlet cloth with a tartan of fine quality.

Donald Roy promised Malcolm that the Prince would be there soon and returned to the inn parlor. As soon as the landlord was out of the room he told the Prince he must go. Charles begged Donald Roy to come with him, saying that he felt safe in the hands of the MacDonalds, but Roy refused because of his foot. He convinced the Prince that he must delay no longer.

69

First there was the business of stowing away the comforts that Kingsburgh had provided for the Prince; a bottle of brandy, four shirts and a cold hen in a napkin were tied to his belt on one side, the bottle of whisky from the inn on the other side. A lump of sugar — sugar came in loaves then and the lump was a substantial one — went into his pocket.

It was perhaps at this time that he gave Flora the garters from his Betty Burke outfit. They must have been Lady Clanranald's best garters, for they were French ones, of blue velvet lined with white silk, with a rhinestone buckle. Flora treasured them long and ultimately had one of the buckles made into a brooch. He paid back to her a slight sum that he had borrowed from her, and he said to her those final words which she — and everyone else connected with the affair — remembered all their lives: "For all that has happened, I hope, Madam, we shall meet at St. James's yet and I will reward you there for what you have done."[16]

Outside in the dark and the rain Malcolm MacLeod was waiting. Donald Roy led the Prince to him, starting out in the opposite direction in case the landlord should be watching and making a circle, and went with them to the boat, where they parted about dawn, July 1, 1746. The little boat set out across the gray water; Donald Roy returned to the inn.

Flora had gone to bed.

Donald Roy was questioned by the innkeeper. He told MacNabb that the gentleman who had just left was Sir John MacDonald, an Irish gentleman who had been skulking among the MacDonalds of Skye and wanted to get home. The landlord said he thought it might have been the Prince, for he looked "very noble" — but when he was questioned by Captain Ferguson nine days later he had no idea at all who the "unknown person" might have been.

⚘ 5 ⚘

The Arrests

THE next morning about ten o'clock Flora and MacEachain left the inn at Portree. They had hoped to get a boat that would take them to Broadford and so save them twenty miles by road, but they were refused. They did find a boat that would set them across Loch Portree, and on the other side they got horses for the forty-four mile ride to Armadale[1] — "a fatiguing journey," Flora said.

Marion MacDonald was surprised to see her daughter, having supposed her to be still at Milton. Saying nothing at all about her adventure with the Prince, Flora gave as her excuse for coming home that South Uist was uncomfortably full of soldiers. Neil MacEachain departed at once to try to rejoin the Prince, and Flora settled down at home with her mother, her half sister Annabella and her three half brothers. For about ten days she was undisturbed.[2]

Though the search for the Prince was still going on furiously in the Long Isle, for the moment Skye itself was quiet. The MacLeod militia had no idea at all that Charles had slipped through their fingers. Donald Roy MacDonald, after reporting to Lady Margaret MacDonald and to Kingsburgh that the Prince had got away to Raasay, spent the night of July first sleeping in the same bed with his old friend Lieutenant MacLeod in the militia's headquarters and was very much relieved to find that MacLeod knew nothing of the Prince's movements.

Charles and Malcolm MacLeod were two nights on Raasay in a "mean, low hut," and Malcolm years later told

Boswell that he heard the Prince, tossing and restless, cry out in his sleep, "Oh, God, poor Scotland!" Beyond bringing them a lamb and a kid in the nook of his plaid, young Raasay seemed to be able to do nothing for them, and on the third day they went back to Skye. All that day and night they tramped across the hills, Charles posing as Malcolm's servant and carrying a bottle of brandy in a bundle, and came on the fourth of July to Strath, MacKinnon's country. The seventy-year-old laird and his young wife received them, and after a merry dinner in a cave the laird and his tacksman of Elgol, John MacKinnon, carried Charles off to the mainland of Scotland in a small boat. Malcolm went back to his home in Raasay.

Meanwhile General Campbell and Captain Ferguson and their soldiers on the Long Island had picked up the scent. One David Campbell, secretary to General Campbell, wrote an account of the search in a letter to a Mr. Maule from Inverary on July 21. "Several of the inhabitants," he wrote,

tho were very averse to give our folks any intelligence but being threatened and afraid of immediate punishment they confessed [that] on Saturday the 28 June the Young Pretender went off in a small boat to the Isle of Skye under the conduct of Miss Mac-Donald, daughter to the Laird of Milton and disguised in women's cloathes as her maid. We got one of the fellows who confessed he rowed them over to Skye and that they landed under Sir Alexander MacDonald's house.[3]

Just as Mrs. MacDonald and Kingsburgh had foreseen.

After capturing Colonel Felix O'Neil and Father Allan MacDonald, they learned that Lady Clanranald had been "all along the Secret Protectress of the Pretender." Pausing long enough to give orders for her arrest, General Campbell set out at once in the *Furnace* with Captain Ferguson for Skye. They went directly to Mugstot.

"Lady Margaret was surprised," continued David Campbell, "when she knew of our errand, told us most frankly upon our inquiry that Miss MacDonald had dined at her house on Sunday the 29th, that though she pressed her to stay all night, yet she could not prevail and that she had a man and maid servant with her. I think her ladyship did not know the maid's quality."

Why, after all, should they suspect Lady Margaret? Her husband was at Fort Augustus with the Duke of Cumberland, and companies of his men were hunting the Prince in the Long Island.

Kingsburgh House was the next stop. Here Captain Ferguson seems to have done the questioning. Mrs. MacDonald told Bishop Forbes about it in July, 1747, and her replies were so spirited and so witty that one cannot help reflecting that the good lady had had thirteen months in which to think of them. She looked Captain Ferguson in the face, she said, and told him, "If Captain Ferguson is to be my judge, then God have mercy on my soul." Ferguson asked why. "Why, sir, the world belies you if you be not a very cruel, hard-hearted man; and indeed I do not like to come into your hands."

After remarking with commendable mildness that people should not believe all that the world says, Ferguson "had the impertinence to ask" Mrs. MacDonald if she had laid the Young Pretender and Miss MacDonald in one bed. To which her answer was: "Sir, whom you mean by the Young Pretender, I shall not pretend to guess; but I can assure you it is not the fashion in the Isle of Skye to lay the mistress and the maid in the same bed together." Ferguson then asked to see the rooms and noticed at once that the maid had had the better one. He said it must have been the Young Pretender in women's clothes. At this point Kingsburgh spoke up and said it could not have been the person he meant for he had heard that person ask something of Miss MacDonald in Erse.[4]

Unfortunately there is nothing at all about this delightful passage in the letter that David Campbell wrote to General Campbell from Portree on July 11. In it he tells of examining Kingsburgh, who told him "upon promise of secrecy that the Prince had gone to Raasay, left there July 3, and come back to Skye with one MacLeod who lives eleven miles from here."

As Kingsburgh was examined by General Campbell himself on board the *Furnace* on the same day, the letter must have been sent along with the prisoner when he was transferred from Portree to the *Furnace,* which was anchored in Applecross Bay on the mainland opposite Raasay. In his examination by General Campbell, Kingsburgh admitted that the Young Chevalier went from his house to Portree with MacEachain and thence to Raasay, and that Miss MacDonald parted with them in Portree. He said that he had no idea how the Prince got a boat to Raasay. It was too late to protect Flora, for her part was already known, but Kingsburgh was careful to keep Donald Roy's name out of it; the names of MacLeod and MacKinnon were not so precious. "The second or third of July the young Chevalier came from Raasay with Malcolm MacLeod who left him in John MacKinnon's house in Arn in MacKinnon's country."[5]

The Young Pretender had eluded his pursuers again, but at least they had the names of those who had helped him to do it. Sending Kingsburgh on to Fort Augustus, they lost no time in going after Flora, Malcolm MacLeod and the MacKinnons. Captain MacLeod of Talisker, a tacksman of MacLeod of MacLeod, who was entrusted with the job, was perhaps all the more determined to catch his prey because his lieutenant had been diddled by them.

On the twelfth of July Donald Roy went to Armadale to see Flora, to tell her about his adventures and to find out what she knew. After spending the night so satisfactorily with Lieutenant MacLeod, he had gone to Mugstot; Lady

Margaret had given him a letter to the Prince, which he had done his best to deliver, following him first to Raasay and then back to Skye and missing him in both places. Along the way he picked up a letter which the Prince had left for him.

Sir — I have parted (I thank God) as intended. Make my compliments to all those to whom I have given trouble — I am, Sir, your humble servant, James Thompson.[6]

Since this is the only written acknowledgement that Charles Edward Stuart ever made to those on the islands who had risked their lives in his behalf, it is worth recording.

On July twelfth, while Donald Roy was at Armadale, Flora received a message from Donald MacDonald of Castleton, another one of her numerous cousins, asking her to come to his house. Uneasy about it, Flora consulted Donald Roy, who suspected a trap and advised her not to comply. When — apparently with the same fatal predilection for danger that sends the heroines of suspense novels out to wander alone through dark deserted passages at midnight — she decided to go in spite of his advice, Donald Roy did what he could to protect her. He asked her to give him her stepfather's letter about Betty Burke, and he primed her with a story to tell in case she was questioned. She was to say that she had seen a great lusty woman who begged a passage in the boat, saying she was a soldier's wife, who went off when they reached Skye.

Flora set off. On the way to Castleton, which was four miles from Armadale, she met her stepfather coming home, but what they said to each other she never told. She went on, but before she reached Castleton she was arrested by an officer and a body of soldiers who had been sent by MacLeod of Talisker. Giving her no chance to go home and tell what had happened or to get a change of clothing, they

carried her off to the *Furnace* in Applecross Bay, where she
was at once taken before General Campbell and questioned.[7]

Campbell himself, though a government man and a
member of the clan long at enmity with the MacDonalds,
was a Highlander; in his relations with the defeated rebels
he was far more moderate than Lowland officers like Ferguson and Scott. To Flora he was throughout kind and just.

In the Public Record Office in London there is a letter
from the Duke of Cumberland to the Duke of Newcastle,
who was Secretary of State, with a postscript dated July 17,
1746, referring to Flora's capture.

Since I had finished my Letter, Captain Hodgson and Sir
Alexander MacDonald are returned from the Isle of Sky and give
me but a bad account of the Pretender's Son's escape, who was
concealed at Sir Alex'r MacDonald's Chief Factor's House, 'till
they got him Safely convey'd to the mainland of Scotland, where
we have him left to hunt. I hope to God that they may take him,
for, else, this Country never will be quiet; & whether it will be so
then, is what I much doubt. I herewith enclose Major General
Campbell's last letter, with the Deposition of the Girl who accompanied him & of another Person's, which will give you the best
Light into the Affair. In the mean time I have seized the Har-
bourer.

Flora's Deposition is as interesting for what she managed
to conceal as for what she actually said.

"Miss MacDonald, daughter-in-law of M'Donald of Milton
in Sky," it begins inaccurately, for she was daughter of the
former Milton, sister of the present one, "being by General
Campbell's order made Prisoner for assisting the eldest son
of the Pretender in his Escape from South Uist, and asked to
declare the circumstances thereof, says, that about six weeks
ago she left her Father-in-law's house at Armadale in Skye
and went South to see some Friends."

Had her rescue of the Prince, she was asked, been arranged before she left Skye? No, she had only heard that he

was somewhere on the Long Island. She described briefly the meeting at the shieling and O'Neil's proposal that the Prince go with her to Skye in women's clothes.

Miss MacDonald says that after this she went and stayed with Lady Clanranald at her House, communicated the scheme to her, and desired that she would furnish cloaths for the Young Pretender as hers would be too little. During Miss MacDonald's stay at Ormaclait [i.e., Nunton] O'Neil came frequently from the Young Pretender to Clan Ranald's home to inform her where he was, what steps had been taken for her voyage and at the same time to hasten her to get her affairs in Readiness for going off.

Step by step they took her through the departure and the crossing to Skye.

The 29th about 11 in the morning they got to Sky near Sir Alexander MacDonald's house. Here Miss MacDonald and Mac-Achran [sic] landed, leaving the Young Pretender in the boat. They went to Sir Alexander MacDonald's house and from thence Miss MacDonald sent for one Donald [Roy] MacDonald, who had been in the Rebellion but had delivered up his arms some time ago. She imployed this Person to procure a boat to carry the Young Pretender to Raasay, after acquainting him with their late voyage and where she had left the Young Pretender. Miss Mac-Donald stayed and dined with Lady Margaret MacDonald, but MacDonald of MacAchran returned to the Boat to inform what was done.

She protected her friends as well as she could. Though she admitted having dined with Lady Margaret, she took on herself the onus of sending for Donald Roy and "imploy"ing him to procure the boat. She said nothing at all of Kingsburgh's being at Mugstot that day.

Miss MacDonald being asked why Raasay was pitched upon for the Young Pretender to retreat to, she answered that it was in

77

hopes of meeting Raasay himself, with whom he was to consult for his future security.

She did her best to take from Kingsburgh the responsibility for having entertained the Prince at his house.

After dinner Miss MacDonald set out for Portree, it being resolved that they should lodge there that night, but on the Road overtook the Young Pretender and MacAchran. They had been joined by MacDonald of Kingsburgh. She told them she must call at Kingsburgh House and desired they would go there also. Here Miss MacDonald was taken sick and therefore with the other two was desired to stay all night, which they agreed to. She had a room to herself, but the Young Pretender and MacAchran lay in the same room. At this time he appeared in woman's cloaths, his face being partly concealed by a Hood or Cloak.

Being asked if while they were at Kingsbury's [sic] House any of the family inquired who the disguised Person was, answers that they did not ask, but that she observed the People of the Family whispering as if they suspected him to be some Person that desired not to be known and from the Servants she found that they suspected him to be MacLeod of Bernera who had been in Rebellion. But being pressed to declare what she knew and believed of Kingsbury's Knowledge of his Guest, owns that she believes he must suspect it was the Young Pretender.

She was then asked where the Young Pretender changed his clothes and what happened at the inn at Portree.

The 30 of June Miss MacDonald set out on Horseback from Kingsbury's House for Portree, having just desired the Young Pretender might put on his own Cloaths somewhere on the road to Portree as she had observed that the other Dress rather made him the more suspected. Miss got to Portree about 12 at night, where she found Donald MacDonald, who had been sent before to procure a Boat. The Young Pretender and MacAchran arrived about an hour later. Here he took some Refreshment, changed a guinea, paid the reckoning, took leave of Miss MacDonald, and went out with Donald MacDonald, but who, after seeing him to the Boat, returned. She believes he went to Raasay, but cannot tell what became of him since.[8]

General Campbell, who must have been impressed by the gentle self-possession of this steadfast young woman, did not release her, but he gave orders that she was to be treated with respect.

John MacKinnon of Elgol was taken and questioned the same day, and two days later MacLeod of Talisker went to Raasay, where Ferguson's men had already burned 300 houses, including the laird's mansion, and 32 boats and slaughtered 280 cows and 700 sheep, and hunted down his friend Malcolm MacLeod in the cow byre where he was hiding, and brought him to the *Furnace*.[9] The old laird of MacKinnon and his wife were captured several days later.

On the day after Flora was taken prisoner, Donald Roy MacDonald and Hugh of Armadale burned the incriminating letters in their possession and took to the hills. Donald Roy had three different caves in which for eight weeks he slept on beds of heather and fern, much plagued by flies and midges. Lady Margaret sent him food and Dr. MacLean sent dressings for his foot. It was perhaps at this time that he had leisure to compose a Latin ode to his wounded foot, which was said by those who presumably knew to be "faultless both in diction and metre." Hugh of Armadale also "skulked" in the heather, hunted with especial diligence by the soliders of General Campbell, who was chagrined at having been outwitted by him. "General Campbell complained to me more than once," said Captain John Hay, of the Customs House Yacht at Ayr, "that MacDonald of Armadale was the man that had misled him when searching for the Young Pretender."[10]

Both Donald Roy and Armadale knew the terrain well

and neither one was ever taken. Armadale had the additional advantage of being known to be a formidable person to tackle.

He is reckoned the strongest man of all the name of Mac-Donald, as I have more than once heard Kingsburgh declare, and his strength of mind seems to bear proportion to the strength of his body. He was obliged for some time to keep out of the way till the suspicion of the passport began to be forgot. But everyone would not have been desirous of the task to lay hands on him; for he never quit his arms when he was skulking and the people of Skye stood in awe of him.[11]

Neither Sir Alexander nor Lady Margaret showed the least concern for Flora, but they were seriously anxious about Kingsburgh, who was in irons at Fort Augustus. They both wrote letters on his behalf to the Lord President Forbes and wrote, it is plain, without consulting each other. Lady Margaret's letter was written first, on July 24, in a hand unusually elegant even for those days.

My Lord:
    Your Lordship can't yet be a stranger to the trouble which has been lately brought upon this Island by the indiscretion of a foolish Girl, with whom the unhappy disturber of this Kingdom landed at this place; tho' I can not but look upon myself and family as peculiarly favoured by Heaven, in drawing that unlucky Visitant so quickly away from the place of his landing that there was no room for considering Him as a Person in Disguise; far less my knowing anything of it.

After this remarkable lapse of memory, she continues:

I must at the same time, not only look upon myself but the whole Country as greatly suffering from the hurt it is likely he has done to the Man into whose House he intruded himself that night; I mean Kingsborrow; a Man well known for his singular honesty, integrity and prudence, in all occurrencies of Life, before that unhappy night, a Man of such consequence and so well liked in this country that if the Pretender's Son had done no other hurt to it but the ruining of this single Man, it could not but render him odious to their Posterity.

Sir Alexander's letter, written from Fort Augustus five days later, told a slightly different story — and gave his wife away.

When the Young Pretender made his unhappy visit to Skye, from South Uist, in a small boat, he landed near my house, in woman's clothes, by way of being maid-servant to one Florence MacDonald, a Girl of Clanranald's family, now a prisoner with General Campbell. Miss MacDonald went and made a visit to Lady Margaret, dined with her, and put her into the utmost distress by telling her of the Cargo that she had brought from Uist. She called on Kingsborrow who was at Mugstot accidentally and they had a very confused consultation together; and it was agreed to hurry him off the Country as fast as possible.

He went on to tell how Charles had played on Kingsburgh's feelings, rain-soaked, pestered by flies and "maigre, ill-colored and eat up by the scab" as he was. Sir Alexander had, he said, pled for Kingsburgh with the Duke of Cumberland "but he stopped my mouth, by saying, that this man had neglected the greatest piece of Service that could have been done; and if he was to be pardoned, you have too much good sense to think this the proper time, as it would encourage others to follow his example."[12]

The letters, so persuasive, did no good. When Kingsburgh was taken from the guardhouse at Fort Augustus, it was only to be transferred to Edinburgh Castle, where he remained until the general amnesty a year later, having suffered, as his friends were quick to point out, a year's imprisonment for a single night's hospitality.

The Duke of Cumberland returned in mid-July to London, where his achievements were heralded with a frenzy of triumph and rejoicing. A ballet entitled "Culloden" was performed at Sadler's Wells; a new dance called the "Culloden Reel" raged everywhere. Handel composed one of his best oratorios, "Judas Maccabeus," in his honor. Tyburn Gate to Hyde Park, where common traitors were hanged, was renamed Cumberland Gate, and an otherwise inoffensive flower had its name changed to Sweet William. There was only one sour note: when the proposal was made to elect the Duke a freeholder of some city company, an alderman, said, "Then let it be of the Butchers."

⚜ 6 ⚜

Prisoner

CONDITIONS on the *Furnace* were bad. Thanks to General Campbell's orders, and because she was a woman, Flora fared well enough, but the other prisoners were crowded together between decks with no candles in the darkness, no beds but coils of rope, and only half rations. Once a day between nine and ten in the morning they were allowed up on the quarter-deck for air and exercise. It was at one of these times that Flora met Colonel Felix O'Neil again.

O'Neil had been taken prisoner just before the *Furnace* left the outer isles and went to Skye. After parting with the Prince and Flora on June 29, he had gone back to South Uist and hunted up O'Sullivan, whom he found sick and exhausted in a cave. With that sharp irony of which history is capable, a French cutter, four days after the Prince had left Benbecula, managed to get through the net of British ships and pick up O'Sullivan and O'Neil. O'Sullivan was saved and so would O'Neil have been, but that he left the cutter to go in search of the Prince, after arranging for the ship to meet him at Loch Seaforth or, if he should not be there, to return after eight days to South Uist for him. Somehow or other this man, who had been considered too conspicuous a foreigner to be seen with Charles and Flora and who had only a two months' acquaintance with parts of the Isles, managed to make his way without being discovered from South Uist to Raasay and from there to Skye and back to South Uist, where he expected to meet O'Sullivan and the French cutter. O'Sullivan, however, had already taken fright and gone off without him. O'Neil, after waiting four days, returned to Benbecula, where he was captured in a shieling near Ross-inish and put aboard the *Furnace.*

Though O'Neil was an officer, Ferguson's fury at losing his royal prey got the better of him and he ordered O'Neil to be stripped, tied to the rack and flogged. Before the actual flogging began, Captain MacCaghan of the Scots Fusiliers stepped in and prevented it. O'Neil had been about a week in the crowded quarters on the *Furnace* when Flora was captured.

The story was told to Bishop Forbes by some of Flora's Edinburgh friends, who had got it from her, that when she met O'Neil on the deck of the *Furnace* she gave him a gentle slap on the cheek, saying lightly, "To that black face do I owe all my misfortune."

To which he is said to have replied, "Why, Madam, what you call your misfortune is truly your greatest honor. And if you'll be careful to demean yourself agreeably to the charac-ter you have already acquired you will in the Event find it to be your Happiness." When she confessed to him her fear of being sent to London and of what might happen to her there, he assured her comfortingly, "You will meet with much respect and very good and great friends for what you have done. Only be careful to make your conduct all of a piece. Never once pretend (through an ill-judged excess of caution and prudence) to repent or be ashamed of what you have done." And he added that he did not the think the government would be so barbarous and cruel as to bring her to a trial for her life.

He often told those who visited him in Edinburgh Castle when he was imprisoned there that he "had been at the same pains as a parent would be with a child to lay down rules to Miss MacDonald for her conduct as a prisoner."[1]

Donald MacLeod of Galtergill, the Prince's faithful helmsman, whose wife was a cousin of Flora's, was also in the hold of the *Furnace,* and so too were Father Allan MacDonald and Malcolm MacLeod, though there is no record of their meeting Flora on the ship. Malcolm MacLeod was fortunate in having friends among the ship's officers who sometimes shared their meals with him.

After Flora had been three weeks on board the *Furnace,* she was transferred to the *Eltham,* Commodore Smith's ship. O'Neil was sent to Edinburgh Castle, and the *Furnace* went on to London to deposit its prisoners in the shocking prison ships anchored off Tilbury Fort. Ferguson, as a reward for his services, was given command of the *Nightingale,* a newly launched frigate of 20 guns. His most notable achievement had been the capture of Simon Fraser, Lord Lovat, the unattractive man who succeeded in being conspicuously a traitor to both sides.[2]

The *Eltham* continued to cruise about the isles for a time. Commodore Thomas Smith, an illegitimate son of Sir Thomas Lyttelton, had been launched into the navy by his baronet father and had risen steadily; commodore in 1746, he became rear admiral in 1747 and Admiral of the Blue ten years later. He was a sensible and moderate man and he took a kindly interest in Flora. Forbes said that "he behaved like a father to her and tendered her many advices as to her behavior in her ticklish situation." Even more welcome and more comforting than his advices, no doubt, was his permitting her to return to her home to see her family and to get some clothes. When the *Eltham* was cruising near Armadale, she was put ashore for two hours with a guard of an officer and a party of soldiers and under promise not to speak Gaelic while she was there. When she came back she brought with her a maid, a girl named Kate MacDonell, who stayed for at least the next few months with her.[3] Kate's presence and devotion must have eased many awkwardnesses for her during the months of imprisonment on shipboard that followed.

There is a tradition that Flora was at Dunstaffnage Castle for a few days, and this may very well be true. Dunstaffnage was one of a chain of five large troop concentrations, which included also Fort Augustus and Fort William. It had stood at the mouth of Loch Etive, four miles from Oban, for centuries and was said to have been the original home of the Stone of Scone.

During the six weeks or so that the *Eltham* spent cruising about before she anchored in Leith Road in early September, Charles Stuart, suffering from abscessive colitis (so his illness was diagnosed in 1960 in a letter in the correspondence column of the *British Medical Journal*) and very much dispirited, was skulking in Glenmoriston, sleeping in caves and hiding in the heather in the rain, eluding capture with luck and by minutes. Neil MacEachain was with him.

The executions of the leaders of the Rebellion began at once, with the beheading of Lords Balmerino and Kilmarnock in July in London, to be followed by that of the Earl of Derwentwater in December and of Lord Lovat the following April. The hanging of 120 others — baronets, clergymen, gentlemen, farmers, laborers — continued through the year. On sunny afternoons, for a pleasant excursion, Londoners sailed down the Thames to Tilbury to look at the ships where rebel prisoners were kept under such appalling conditions that in the first three months 157 out of 564 had died.

On the seventh of September the *Eltham* anchored in Leith Road. Flora was soon transferred to the *Bridgewater*, of which Charles Knowles, later to be Admiral Sir Charles Knowles, was captain. In him Flora found another polite and sympathetic jailor. She was never once, during the two months that the *Bridgewater* remained at Leith, permitted to leave the ship, but she had a comfortable cabin and she was allowed to have all the company that she wanted.

Leith was an old city, separate then from Edinburgh, into which it has now been absorbed, a town of tall stone

houses with crowstepped gables and a wide view of the
Firth of Forth. From Edinburgh on its heights three or four
miles away the Jacobite ladies came trooping down to see
the famous prisoner. The Duke of Cumberland had complained in June, "The Jacobite ladies at Edinburgh went in
Procession in new Plaids and White Cockades to visit their
Prisoner Friends in Edinburgh Castle. Surely these People
are more perverse and stiff-necked than the Jews." Three
months had in no way abated their enthusiasm; they came to
see Flora bearing gifts, they drank tea in the cabin and
danced — no doubt the presence of young officers was an
added attraction — and though professing to be disappointed because they could never persuade Flora to join in
the dance, they admired her gravity.

Some of their names still live. Miss Rachel Houston, who
was later to marry Bishop Forbes, inquired if Flora had any
books to read. When she said she had only a prayer book,
Rachel came again with a Bible in two pretty pocket volumes, handsomely bound. Lady Mary Cochrane, the daughter of the Countess of Dundonald, was with Flora one day
when a squall came up and made the sea so rough that it
was not easy to row a small boat to the dock. Lady Mary
whispered to Flora that she would like to stay on board all
night so that she could say she had the honor of sleeping in
the same bed with the person who had been so happy as to
be the guardian of the Prince. Flora agreed and Lady Mary
enjoyed this signal honor.

They were all enchanted with Flora's stories of those two
days with the Prince and rapturous over the Prince's care for
Flora. They found Flora herself charming and surprisingly
poised for one who had come from those remote and savage
islands, and they praised her behavior as "easy, modest and
well-adjusted" — a curiously modern phrase. "She has a
sweet voice and sings well; and no lady, Edinburgh-bred,
can acquit herself better at the tea-table than what she did

in Leith Road."[4] A lady's performance at the tea table was important; thirty years later Dr. Johnson was very critical of Lady MacDonald, Lady Margaret's daughter-in-law, both for her dull and heavy conversation at tea — "She would sink a ninety-gun ship," he said ungallantly — and for her tea-table appointments, which lacked tongs or even super-numerary spoons, so that he had to take his sugar in his fingers.

One of the young officers on both the *Eltham* and the *Bridgewater* was Nigel Gresley, later Sir Nigel, who was so kind to Flora that when in 1747 she had her portrait painted by Richard Wilson she gave it to Gresley in return for all he had done for her.

The oldest and most important of her friends was Lady Bruce, the seventy-six-year-old widow of Sir William Bruce of Kinross, who lived at the Citadel of Leith and made her home a center for Jacobites, from which she dispensed hospitality and if necessary money. A generous contributor to Charles's cause, she was suspected of harboring him, and her house was searched on September twenty-eighth. There must have been a good deal of bustle and talk about the search, for word reached Flora on the *Bridgewater* that the Prince had been captured, and she was much distressed that all her efforts had been made useless. Actually, however, he had been picked up at Arisaig on September thirteenth by a French man-of-war and was safe in Brittany. Lady Bruce came often to see Flora and brought her the most imagina-tive of the gifts she received — linen, cambric, a thimble, needles and thread, so that she could fill some of the long dull hours with sewing — a contrast to Commodore Smith's generous but at the moment tactless present of a handsome suit of riding clothes.

She was allowed to write letters at this time, but none of her letters have survived. Bishop Forbes refers to one that she wrote home to Armadale begging the family to take care of the Prince's garters for her, "for she put a great value on them." Later, while she was in London, her half brother James, on his way to Holland to take service in the Dutch army, stopped at Leith and gave the garters to Lady Bruce to keep for Flora.

At length, early in November, the *Bridgewater* was ordered to London and Flora perforce went with her. On the twentieth they reached the Nore, at the mouth of the Thames, where the *Bridgewater* was to go into dock. There were no orders about Flora, and Captain Knowles was in a quandary. A letter from him asking for direction survives; there is no address to show to whom it was written but almost certainly it was to Commodore Smith. It was dated from the *Bridgewater*, November 30.

Sir:

Miss Flora MacDonald is arriv'd here with me and as she esteems you her best friend (s)he has in the world should be much obliged if you'd be pleased to let her know what is to become of her. I have wrote to the Admiralty about her but as it may be some time before it may be settled, as their Lord-ships will first send to the Secretary of State we may possibly go into the Dock before that time and she be sent on board the *Royal Sovereign,* which would not be very agreeable to her. Therefore I should be glad (if) there could be an order got for her being sent up to London as soon as possible. Miss joyns me in Respects.[5]

Knowles, who was forty-five at the time, was a pleasant-looking man with large melancholy eyes, somewhat long in the nose and short in the chin; he went on to rise in his career, becoming an admiral at fifty-six and a baronet seven years later. He and Commodore Smith had worked closely together during the 'Forty-five, intercepting many small French vessels which were attempting to take aid and supplies to the rebels.

He was not able to save Flora from a brief period on the *Royal Sovereign,* an old and large ship-of-war — 100 guns — used as a prison ship, but after a few days the orders came through and she was taken to London, tradition says to the Tower. There is no record of this, however, and it is highly unlikely. General Williamson, the Lieutenant Governor of the Tower at that time, did not want ordinary prisoners; he preferred to harbor only the titled and aristocratic — and rich. The Duke of Atholl died there in July, 1746; the four peers who were beheaded lodged in the Tower before they went to their deaths. Lord and Lady Traquair had quarters in the Lieutenant Governor's own house and complained of the seven guineas a week that they had to pay for their comforts. But the Duke of Atholl had paid ten guineas.

Flora, like other prisoners of quality but not great importance, was lodged in a "messenger's house." Messengers were government officials who escorted prisoners and witnesses from one place to another and sometimes carried mail. They were permitted to turn their own houses into private gaols for profit. There were five or six of them at this time who did this and some of them made a very good thing out of it, charging their guests high and crowding them into garrets and cellars and feeding them little and badly. Mr. William Dick, who in July had been carrying letters back and forth between Cumberland in Fort Augustus and Newcastle at Whitehall, ran one of the best of the houses, and a messenger named Carrington was known as the worst and most hated of them. Even with all their disadvantages, the messengers' houses were very much desired by those prisoners unfortunate enough to be consigned to Newgate, the New Gaol, Southwark, and elsewhere.

Flora was taken to Mr. Dick's on December 6, and there she found others already settled in. Malcolm MacLeod, after several months on a transport at Tilbury Fort, had been moved to Mr. Dick's a month before; Clanranald was there, though Lady Clanranald was not permitted to be in the same house with her husband; Aeneas MacDonald, the banker; MacDonald of Boisdale, who had actually kept Clanranald's men in the Isles from joining the Rebellion and whose only crime was that he had visited Charles in Glen Corradale and given him brandy; and Dr. Burton of York. Robert Burton was a physician who, when the Prince had marched into England, had announced his intention of going to kiss his hand. He never succeeded in performing this act of enthusiasm, for he was arrested in November, 1745, imprisoned for three months in York Castle and then removed to Mr. Dick's house in London, where he was held until March 27, 1747. He and Flora became fast friends.

There were others too, for shorter or longer periods, the Prince's barber and wigmaker, three ensigns, Donald Mac-Leod of Galtergill, and the laird of MacKinnon, who had been first in a prison ship at Tilbury where, said Donald MacLeod, the MacKinnon "held out wonderfully though a man upwards of seventy." Lady MacKinnon was confined at Messenger Munie's in Derby Court, Westminster, where she was crowded with a number of others into a cockloft with a hole in the roof for light and a rotten floor, no stoves or heat of any kind. She survived, however, to bear her elderly husband three children after they finally got back to Skye.

While Flora had been on the *Bridgewater* on her way to London, Sir Alexander MacDonald of Sleat had also decided to go to London in order to join the Duke of Cumberland. He left Skye, stopped at the barracks of Glenelg in Bernera, just across from Kylerhea in Skye, and there was stricken and died on November 23. It was said by some that his grief over the cruelties after Culloden had undermined his health, but a bitter and unforgiving little quatrain went about:

> *If Heaven is pleased when sinners cease to sin,*
> *If Hell is pleased when sinners enter in,*
> *If Earth is pleased, freed of a truckling knave,*
> *Then all are pleased — MacDonald's in his grave.*

He was succeeded as chief by his five-year-old son James, and the following July a posthumous son was born to Lady Margaret.

London in 1746 and 1747 was no more than a town by modern standards, but it was the largest city in the west at that time. The fashionable world had already spilled over into Mayfair; Berkeley Square and Grosvenor Square were filling up, and the streets that ran down to Piccadilly. St. James's Piccadilly was the most fashionable church to attend. The King, now a widower, lived in St. James's Palace with his mistresses. His eldest son, Frederick, Prince of Wales, whom he detested and who returned the sentiment, lived in Leicester Square, where also lodged Hogarth, whose series of prints, "Marriage à la Mode," had appeared in 1745 and whose portrait of Lord Lovat of the evil face and sprawling body was all the rage in 1746, sold everywhere in all kinds of forms, including watch papers, those thin small bits of paper that went inside the covers of watches to protect the face.

Everybody bought Hogarth prints, everybody went to Covent Garden to hear operas and oratorios by Handel, everybody went to plays at Drury Lane Theater, of which Garrick had just become manager. The literary men met at coffeehouses and talked by the hour. Fielding was writing *Tom Jones,* Smollett, *Roderick Random,* both of which were published in 1748. Dr. Johnson was at work on his dictionary and was so quiet in 1745 and 1746 that some people have suggested that he was actually out in the 'Forty-five. Boswell was a child of six living at Auchinleck House in Ayrshire, the home of his father, "a respectable judge."

The frenzy of rejoicing over the defeat of the Rebellion, like the hysteria of fear that had preceded it, had died down, and the Jacobites in London raised their heads again and talked quietly among themselves about the possibility of another try later. As at Leith, there was a titled Jacobite who encouraged and befriended Flora.

Lady Primrose was the young widow of Hugh Primrose, third viscount, and the daughter of Peter Drelincourt, dean of the Anglican cathedral at Armagh in Ireland. She lived in one of a row of seventeenth-century houses in Essex Street, which ran down from the Strand to the Thames, and her home was the headquarters, then and later, for the ruined but still hopeful Jacobite movement. She not only visited Flora at Mr. Dick's and later entertained her at her house but she raised a purse for her which amounted to fifteen hundred pounds, a by no means inconsiderable sum in the currency of those days.

The story is told that Flora was also visited by Frederick, Prince of Wales, who liked to do anything to annoy his brother Cumberland, with whom he was on as bad terms as he was with his father, George II. She is supposed to have said to him that she would have done the same thing for him as she did for Charles, if he had been in like distress.

During that year two pamphlets were published in which Flora figured. One, by a J. Drummond, was entitled, "The Female Rebels, 1747. Being Some Remarkable Incidents of the Lives, Characters and Families of the Titular Duke and Duchess of Perth, the Lord and Lady Ogilvie and of Miss Flora M'Donald." It had a great deal to cover in its sixty-two pages — with considerable moralizing thrown in — and so not surprisingly the part devoted to particulars of the "Life, Family and Character of Miss Florence M'Donald, now in custody of one of His Majesty's Messengers in London, on Suspicion of Treasonable Practices against the Government" was meager. Most interesting is its description of her as "a young lady about twenty" — she was by now close to twenty-six — "of graceful person, good complexion, and peculiar sweetness mixed with majesty in her countenance," and its comments on her great calm, unruffled in confinement. The writer, who was staunchly loyal to the government and disapproved thoroughly of Lady Perth and Lady Ogilvie, excused Flora for her disloyalty on the grounds of her womanly kind heart.

The other pamphlet, which called itself a novel, was even shorter; *Alexis: or, the Young Adventurer*, published in London in 1746, was only thirty-three pages long. It took the form of a pastoral, in which Alexis, "a shepherd of the first rank on the continent of Robustia," came to rescue the lower shepherds from the miseries into which they had sunk, suffered defeat at the battle of Lachrymania, skulked in the islands and was carried to safety by a lovely young girl named Heroica, with the aid of Honorius her stepfather and Fidelius of Regicia. Heroica is described as "blessed with a Greatness of Soul and Happiness of Invention far superior to most of her tender Years," and, lest the meaning should escape anyone, a key to the names was provided. Besides the obvious characters, Clarinda was Lady Clanranald; Veracious, Neil MacEachain; Deceptus, Sir A. MacDonald; Constantius, Captain MacLeod; Militarius, General C — mpb — l; Sa — gui — ius, Some Butchering Fellow; Aetheria, the Isle of Skye; Blood-Hounds, the Army. The writer evidently had some sympathy for the MacLeods, for they were named Erronei, and a touch of humor, for the "Highland language" was Yalk. It told the story of the Prince's escape from Benbecula to Skye for the most part accurately, though it gave Flora credit for masterminding the whole scheme. There was a vivid account of the horrors after Culloden and a circumstantial description of Kingsburgh's finding the Prince by the running sheep and also details of his capture and the treatment of him afterwards. The story ended abruptly with Alexis hiding on the mainland of Robustia — probably because that was where he was when the story was written.

It was published anonymously, and even Bishop Forbes

was never certain who was the author, though he records that Kingsburgh said it was so exact that only he or Neil MacEachain could have written it. MacEachain, however, was skulking himself at the time; Kingsburgh was in Edinburgh Castle under the strictest guard. There was one other person who could have known the facts directly from Kingsburgh, who had something of a literary turn and who later at any rate had a tenderness for Flora, and that was Kingsburgh's son Allan, then a lieutenant of the militia.

Flora at Messenger Dick's evidently enjoyed a good deal of freedom. She was courted by the London Jacobites and seems to have been able to accept their hospitality. Thomas Pennant, the travel writer, seizing the opportunity to drop two names at once, spoke of having met her in 1746 at Sir Watkin William Wynne's. In April, 1747, she was about to go on a pleasure jaunt to Windsor with Aeneas MacDonald when her escort was suddenly arrested and taken off to Newgate Prison, where he complained of the vermin and said that he would gladly pay six shillings eight pence a day at a messenger's house. Presumably that is what Flora paid, out of the purse collected for her by Lady Primrose.

On the fourth of July, 1747, a general amnesty was declared and the Jacobite prisoners were immediately set free, Kingsburgh in Edinburgh, Lady MacKinnon, Boisdale, the Clanranalds, Malcolm MacLeod, Donald of Galtergill and others in London. Flora's release, for some reason, did not come for several days. She had had a year of imprisonment without ever being brought to trial or even charged. The laird of MacKinnon was held for two more years.

Evidently when Flora left Mr. Dick's house she went to stay with Lady Primrose, who arranged for her to travel northward in the most luxurious way then available, by post chaise. There was at that time a stagecoach which went once a month from London to Edinburgh and took twelve days for the trip; people made their wills before setting out. A chaise could do the journey in six days. Asked to select an escort for the journey, Flora chose Malcolm MacLeod and so gave him the line that he was to repeat with satisfaction all his life and which was to endow him with the little fame he had:

"So I went to London to be hanged and came down in a chaise with Miss Flora MacDonald."[6]

To avoid attention "from the mob" on the way — for Flora was famous — they traveled as Miss Robertson and her brother.

The Duke of Cumberland

PORTRAIT BY SIR JOSHUA REYNOLDS

Charles Edward Stuart in his old age

PORTRAIT BY H. D. HAMILTON

≈ 7 ≈

Marriage

FLORA and Malcolm MacLeod reached Edinburgh on the second of August, having stopped over in York to see Dr. Burton. Flora stayed in Edinburgh until the following April. She had friends there now and she was set, furthermore, on improving her handwriting. A clear hand in those days before typewriters was a necessity for any man who wanted to get on in the world, and an elegant one was the mark of a lady. Flora evidently felt at a disadvantage with hers, and she lost no time in making arrangements for lessons.

David Beatt, a Jacobite schoolmaster, wrote to a friend, "As I have entered with Miss Flory MacDonald, who waited five weeks for my return to town and who needs very much to be advanced in her writing, confines me to daily attendance and must do so till she is brought to some length in it, which obliges me to keep the Town close."[1]

Kingsburgh, who was released from Edinburgh Castle on July fourth, had gone back to Skye. His wife had come to Edinburgh to be near him, even though for weeks she could not visit him in the Castle but had to stand outside in the parade ground and shout up to the window where he stood behind bars. Not till after he was taken ill had she been permitted to see him in his room. They had lingered in Edinburgh, after he was freed, long enough to talk twice with Mr. Forbes before they left, but they were gone before Flora reached there. Malcolm MacLeod stayed on in Edinburgh for several months before he went back to Brea; his money

97

ran short and the Jacobites raised a purse for him and sent him on his way in January.

In November Dr. Burton came to Edinburgh, expressly to make inquiries about the Prince's affairs and to exchange information with Mr. Forbes. Burton had already taken down a "Journal" from Flora's lips, which he gave to Mr. Forbes, and Forbes had written out several questions which he wanted Burton to ask Flora. How had she happened to meet Colonel O'Neil? Had the Prince any private meeting with Armadale while skulking? What songs did he sing in crossing from the Long Isle? and the like. Flora answered them, and the doctor gave the answers in writing to Forbes.

It was not till January of 1748 that Flora and Forbes met. Then they both dined at Lady Bruce's house in the Citadel of Leith with several others, including Donald Roy Mac-Donald, who had come to Edinburgh at Kingsburgh's "express desire" to talk with Forbes. Flora and Donald Roy both talked freely of their experiences and answered questions. Donald's foot was by this time entirely well again; he had walked from Skye to Edinburgh in twelve days.

In March Flora was again at Lady Bruce's talking to Forbes. He showed her the copy of Armadale's letter that Donald Roy had given him, for her to correct, and she added a sentence that had been omitted.

The Reverend Robert Forbes, who was in his late thirties at this time, was the rector of the Episcopal church in Leith and a wholehearted Jacobite who had done his best to strike a blow for Charles. When the news came in September, 1745, that the Prince had landed, Forbes with two other clergymen and four friends set out at once to join him. They were caught at St. Ninians near Stirling and thrown into Stirling Castle, where they were held prisoner till February, 1746, when they were transferred to Edinburgh Castle. As he talked to other prisoners and heard their stories, he was seized with the idea of gathering firsthand accounts from all who had had any part in the Rebellion and preserving them for posterity.

When he was released from Edinburgh Castle, in June, 1746, he started in at once. At this time Lady Bruce invited him to stay in her house at the Citadel of Leith, and she helped him in his undertaking by entertaining people there who had stories to tell. Forbes would ask them questions and write down what they said, then give them the account afterwards to check and correct. He was partisan in his sympathy but he attempted also to be scrupulously accurate. When two accounts of the same event did not gibe, he was off hotfoot to question the participants again or to get a third account from another eyewitness. He weighed and estimated the value of the narratives; he added later corrections and emendations in footnotes. When he could not get the original of a statement that he wanted, he acquired a copy and had the copy certified. Felix O'Neil, for instance, wrote a "Journal" of his experiences and gave the original to the Countess of Dundonald, who insisted on keeping it herself. Various copies were circulated but Forbes could not rest until he had got a loan of the original and compared his copy with it. His one failure was Armadale. He made repeated efforts to get a statement from him, but that wary gentleman, who had skulked so successfully, had no intention of committing himself in writing.

For several years Forbes gathered this material together, 1,598 pages of it, which he had bound in nine octavo volumes covered in black leather, the pages edged with black and a broad border of black around the nine title pages. Any mementos that he could collect were fastened to it. Flora gave him a piece of the Prince's garter and a bit of tape from his Betty Burke apron (she brought the whole apron to Edinburgh on a later trip and gave Mr. Forbes the thrill of tying it around him), and Mrs. MacDonald of Kingsburgh sent him a bit of the sprigged linen dress and a snip of tartan from the waistcoat which Kingsburgh gave Charles and which he later exchanged with Malcolm Mac-Leod for a commoner one. Forbes entitled his collection *The Lyon in Mourning*, the lion being Scotland's heraldic device, and as long as he lived he refused to publish it. In 1834 it came into the hands of Sir Robert Chambers, the historian, who incorporated parts of it in his *Jacobite Memoirs* and drew on the whole of it for his *History of the Rebellion*. He bequeathed it to the Faculty of Advocates in Edinburgh, and it is now in the National Library of Scotland. In 1896 the Scottish History Society edited the whole and published it in three large volumes in its series of publications.

Robert Forbes, when Flora first knew him, was a bachelor, but in 1749 he married Agnes Gairey, who died within a few months, and, some time after, Flora's friend Rachel Houston. In 1762 he was appointed Bishop of Caithness.

The character of the man comes through the pages of his monumental work: eager, warmhearted, insatiably curious, indefatigable, persevering. His feeling for the Prince was one of romantic loyalty; for Flora he had a tender admiration; for Kingsburgh, respect and affection. He had little interest in the larger issues; it was the human drama that captivated him, and perhaps in the end most of all he was caught up by the collector's passion for completeness. No detail was too small: he saved every letter, every scrap of paper — Donald Roy's Latin verses on Jacobite subjects which kept coming long after Donald Roy had settled down as a schoolmaster in North Uist; a Latin poem on Flora written by Dr. John King, principal of St. Mary's, Oxford; all the voluminous correspondence with others involved in the search, in which they exchanged news of whom they had seen and when and what they were doing now. He obviously enjoyed the fellowship and the activity, even after all the material was in and there was nothing more to learn.

It is through Forbes that we know that in April, 1748,

Flora set out at last for Skye. She and her friend Peggy Callander went first to Argyllshire, were no doubt Flora spent some time with the Largie cousins. In July Mr. Forbes wrote to Dr. Burton that he had heard that Flora was almost drowned when the ferryboat on which she was crossing to Argyllshire struck a rock, "but (under God) a clever Highlander saved her."[2]

Dr. Burton was closer to Flora than Bishop Forbes; he saw her more often and heard from her directly and could usually give Mr. Forbes information about her. "I received a line from Miss F. M'D.," he wrote in July, 1748, "telling me she was just going to visit her friends in the west and should not return to Edinburgh till Stepember when she intends to favor me with her company at York on her way to London."[3]

She went to London, partly to see about the money that was held for her there, and in the winter of 1750 she was back again in Edinburgh, talking to Mr. Forbes at the end of March, when she gave him the names of the boatmen who had rowed the Prince from Benbecula to Skye.

That summer she returned to Armadale, and Mr. Forbes wrote her a letter of condolence for the "affecting loss of two hopeful youths," the half brothers whose names were never told.

She was not in London in 1750 when Charles Edward Stuart made his secret visit there.

After leaving Scotland in September, 1746, Charles had gone to Paris to ask with unquenchable optimism for a large expedition to Scotland. Louis XV offered him a pension instead, which he refused. After a fruitless trip to Spain to try to enlist the help of the royal family there, he returned to Paris, where he was soon in trouble on account of his affairs with women. Forced to retire to Avignon, he stayed there until February, 1749, when he left and began his years of wandering over the face of Europe. For a week in September, 1750, he was in London, probably in concealment at

Lady Primrose's.[4] While he was there, he renounced his Catholicism and joined the Church of England "in the new church in the Strand,"* but as his conversion was never announced to the British people it failed to win him the sympathy and support which was probably its purpose. He visited the Tower of London and thought the gate might be blown up with a petard; he met about fifty of his followers, including the Duke of Beaufort and the Earl of Westmoreland — or so he told Gustavus of Sweden more than thirty years later — in a room in Pall Mall. Raasay's younger brother, Dr. Murdoch MacLeod, told Boswell in 1773 that Charles's plan had been to seize the royal family and put them aboard a ship, after which he would proclaim his father King at Charing Cross. It all came to nothing. It is likely that the government knew that he was there but by this time considered him negligible.

Probably Flora knew nothing about all this. She was occupied with something of far greater importance to her: she was preparing for her marriage to Kingsburgh's elder son.

Allan MacDonald was a tall, well-built, handsome man with black hair, a high nose and large, widely spaced eyes — vigorous, active, intelligent but not reflective. He had begun his education with the local schoolmaster and finished it in Edinburgh at Sir Alexander MacDonald's expense.[5] In 1745 and 1746 he had been a lieutenant in an independent company under the Duke of Cumberland and Lord Loudon, but when the militia was disbanded he was not in line for half pay, a circumstance he spoke of with some soreness more than thirty years later. Like so many young Highlanders he would have liked a military career, and Lady Margaret MacDonald tried to get him a commission in the regiment that was then being raised for the Dutch service — perhaps

* Either St. Clement Danes or St. Mary le Strand.

the same regiment that Flora's brother James actually managed to get into — but as there was evidently no opening for Allan, he resigned himself to becoming a tacksman of his young chief, Sir James, who was by now a serious and lovable small boy of eight.

Kingsburgh's handsome son and Flora, now twenty-eight, charming, famous, with some money of her own, were a well-matched couple; probably they were in love. Certainly the marriage was a devoted one. The wedding took place at Armadale on November 6, 1750, with Flora, who was in mourning for her two younger brothers, wearing a black silk gown.

A little less than a month after they were married, the marriage contract was drawn up, by the same Dr. John MacLean who had taken care of Donald Roy after Culloden, and signed by the young couple.[6] It filled five pages of "stampt paper" with legal terminology and scarcely a punctuation mark, but the salient points of it were that Flora, called "Flory" throughout, was to have fifty pounds a year and that she was to transfer to Allan her fortune of seven hundred pounds sterling, then lying in the hands of certain trustees and friends in England. The witnesses to the contract, besides Kingsburgh and Dr. MacLean, were Hugh MacDonald of Armadale and Donald MacDonald of Castleton, the cousin whom she had been on her way to see the day she was arrested four years earlier.

Kingsburgh wrote to Mr. Forbes on New Year's Eve about the "new marryed couple" and added with a touch of pride, "My ribb and I offers you our kind service as does my son and daughter." Forbes was hurt that Flora had not written him herself, as his reply to Kingsburgh shows: "Pray make an offer of my best wishes in the kindest manner to my worthy Mrs. Flora MacDonald and tell her from me that I looked for some lines under her own hand to let me know about her marriage day, which I and some others are quite ignorant about."[7] He hastened to write to Dr. Burton, who replied, "I heartily wish my worthy Flora as happy as it is possible to be this side the grave, and that she may live to see her children's children so too; and also peace upon Israel, which God grant that we may soon see and be saved. Amen."

The *Scots Magazine*, which did not report many marriages, took note of this one:

"Nov. 6 at Armadale in Sleat. Allan MacDonald, eldest son of Alexander MacDonald of Kingsburgh, to Miss Flora Mac-Donald, daughter of Ranald MacDonald of Milton, deceas'd. This is the young lady who aided the escape of the young Chevalier."

8

The Family Grows

FLORA and Allan lived at Kingsburgh for the first few months after they were married until, at Whitsuntide in 1751, the tack of Flodigarry became vacant and Allan acquired it, using to pay for tack and cattle the money that Flora brought to him on their marriage, to which Lady Primrose seems to have added something more at this time.[1] Flodigarry was on the northeastern tip of Trotternish. There is a house there still, long and low, of whitewashed stone with a thatched roof, known as Flora MacDonald's cottage. Behind it rises the northernmost of the mountains of Trotternish, crowned with that dramatically shaped formation of rocks called the Quirang; to the east, across the Minch, the mountains of Ross reach up into the sky. In the eighteenth century the Scottish scenery was generally considered much too wild and rugged for beauty — "a wide extent of hopeless sterility," said Johnson, and "a uniformity of barrenness" — but beautiful it was, and whether or not Flora was conscious of it her spirit must have been fed by it. When, years later, she found herself in a flat, hot country, surrounded by longleaf pines, she must have missed beyond telling those cold, misty, ineffably lovely mountains of western Scotland.

In this little house during the next nine years her first five children were born: Charles (surely named for the Prince) in 1751, Anne in 1754, Alexander in 1755, Ranald in 1756, James in 1757.

During the years that they spent at Flodigarry, Allan was busy with the farm and his tenants, with hunting and fishing; Flora with the babies. Small and crowded as the house was there would be servants to help, and the young couple would be free to take part in whatever social life the island afforded: visits from relatives, or an occasional funeral or wedding, which would draw people from the other islands and from the mainland as well. Funerals were almost as festive as weddings, for after the long procession to the graveyard was over a great feast followed, with whole roast sheep or oxen and gallons of whisky.

Flora's half sister Annabella was married to Alexander MacDonald of Cuidreach, one of the tacks belonging to the young chief, Sir James MacDonald of Sleat, and there must have been a large gathering of the family at Armadale for that. Sometime before 1771, it is not known when, Marion MacDonald, Flora's mother, died, and the family and friends would have rallied round for her funeral.

The business of selling the black cattle raised at Flodigarry would take Allan to Edinburgh from time to time, and Flora seems to have gone to visit her cousins at Largie.

Housekeeping in those remote islands was difficult. There were no shops of any kind in Skye. Peddlers came at long intervals with such small wares as they could carry in packs on their backs or fastened to the saddle of a horse. In an almost treeless land there was no wood for fuel or for making the small useful things that in other places were taken for granted. Fires were lit and houses warmed with the peat that was cut and stacked on the moors, but when a wooden "coggie," a vessel made like a miniature barrel, leaked beyond repair, a replacement could not be fashioned on the spot by a handy man in the household. Slowly and with difficulty manufactured articles did reach the houses of the islands, by ship and by road; furniture, plate, books were accumulated but only through the expense of time and thought and patience as well as money. Tea, coffee, sugar and spices had to be imported, and though whisky could be made locally the claret which was the gentleman's drink must come from the mainland. Most of their food was produced in the thin, stony soil of the island.

The peasants who rented crofts from the tacksmen had a monotonous diet: oatmeal and milk and cheese; meat only occasionally when someone slaughtered a sheep. In bad times the thin cattle were bled and the blood mixed with milk and oatmeal to make a sort of cake. The tacksmen, however, ate well, and for the most part on well-appointed tables. Their ladies took pride in their linen tablecloths, their silver dishes and their queen's ware. In a day when an ample figure was considered attractive and nobody counted calories, one kind of meat or dessert for a meal was not enough; tables were spread with platters of game (muirfowl, venison), fish, beef, mutton, chicken; there was plenty of milk and eggs for sillabubs and puddings; there was marmalade and honey, cheese, oatcakes—but little white bread, for wheat did not do well in the islands; for vegetables they had potatoes and turnips. Always there was punch to drink, as well as claret, whisky and brandy. When Dr. Johnson visited Skye, his hosts were able to produce lemons for the lemonade that he habitually drank.

In 1755 Kingsburgh, who was by then seventy-five years old, resigned the office of factor and Allan succeeded him in this position. When the young laird came of age a few years later, Kingsburgh was given an annuity of fifty pounds a year and a citation which Boswell recorded.

I Sir James Macdonald of Macdonald, Baronet, now, after arriving at my perfect age, from the friendship I bear to Alexander Macdonald of Kingsburgh, and in return for the long and faithful services done and performed by him to my deceased father, and to myself during my minority, when he was one of my tutors and curators; being resolved, now that the said Alexander MacDonald is advanced in years, to contribute my endeavors for making his old age placid and comfortable — [2]

In 1756 Kingsburgh's wife died, and Flora and Allan with their children moved to Kingsburgh House to live there and take care of the old gentleman. Allan carried on the tack for his father. Two more children were born here, John, who was to be the most successful and the best known of Flora's five sons, in the autumn of 1759, and Frances, or Fanny, the baby of the family, nearly seven years later, in 1766.

In the same year in which Frances was born, Sir James MacDonald, the well-loved young chief, died in Rome in his twenty-fifth year. He was one of those handsome, brilliant, serious young men whose early death in the spring of their promise brings such sorrow to their family and friends and a sense of loss even to those who read about them later. After Eton and Oxford, he had gone on the grand tour in Europe with the young Duke of Buccleuch under the tutorship of Professor Adam Smith of Edinburgh University, later to be famous as the author of *The Wealth of Nations*. Sir James won the admiration of the French court for his learning and the nickname of "the Scottish Marcellus." Returning to Skye, he had set himself to administering his estates with a concern for the welfare of his people that endeared him to them all. Injured in a shooting accident — by that same MacLeod of Talisker who had been responsible for the arrest of Flora and of Malcolm MacLeod in 1746 — he had gone to Italy for his health and died in Rome in 1766. In him Flora and Allan lost a valuable friend; if he had lived, the whole course of their subsequent lives might have been different, for his younger brother Alexander, who succeeded him as chief, was a different sort of man altogether, interested in his Skye estates only as a source of income.

Even before Sir James's death, however, Allan was in difficulties. Like many other Highlanders of his class and time, he was a soldier, a reader, a gentleman, but no businessman and not much of a farmer. At the end of the eleven years during which he served as factor to the MacDonald estates in Skye, he was deep in debt, both to the laird and to others. Boswell tells us that Raasay had lent Allan five hundred pounds, no small sum then.

A long letter which he wrote in January, 1767, to John MacKenzie of Delvine, the Edinburgh law agent for the barony of MacDonald and good friend to all the family, reveals much of Allan's character, his circumstances and his way of life.

He begins by admitting that he had annoyed Mr. Mac-Kenzie by leaving Edinburgh on a recent trip without seeing him as he should have done, but gives as his excuse, rather ingenuously, that since he was already in Mr. MacKenzie's bad graces he had preferred to avoid him. He confesses to foolish conduct in the past but insists that it had injured only himself and his family. His intentions were always honest and his troubles were not of his own making but were due to ill luck and to the "groundless backbiteings" of "evil wishers." He had wished, he says, to resign the factorship when he was in a position to repay the arrears he owed his master, but he had not been permitted to do so. A year or two later, after he had overextended himself by the purchase of 2,800 cattle, his resignation was called for, and also the money which he owed and at that point could not pay. He does not blame his "dear deceased master" for this injustice but ascribes it to Sir James's ignorance of the economics of the island and his misplaced confidence in men of "weake parts and enveyous temper."

The purpose of writing the letter was to ask Mr. Mac-Kenzie to use his influence with the new chief to renew the lease of the tack of Kingsburgh. He hoped, he said, to be able to pay the money that he owed in the following April — but only if interest was not demanded of him.

It was the letter of a harried, muddled man trapped in a system which was proving disastrous to abler men than he.

Through the letter comes a glimpse of what the life of a

tacksman was. His wealth was in cattle, which were driven to the mainland to be sold. Business required him to go from time to time to Edinburgh, an expensive trip and a long and difficult one in the days when there was no proper road north of Inverness. We see Allan in his difficulties going to his father for advice and also to Flora's stepfather, Hugh of Armadale. We see him anxious to educate his five sons and so to put them in the way of doing something for themselves. He had incurred criticism, he said, by trying to wangle a lieutenancy for his eldest son, Charles, when Charles was no more than a child. He was afraid that Mr. MacKenzie would think his father's annuity of fifty pounds should be of help to him, but for reasons not clear from the letter old Kingsburgh did not get all of the fifty pounds and the amount he paid for board and lodging for himself and his servant was only fourteen pounds four shillings a year — though, Allan hastened to say, if he paid nothing at all he would be "excessive welcome."[3]

The lease of the tack was in the end renewed but at a greatly increased rent. Allan accepted the increase in rent — what else could he do? — and prepared to go ahead with some "little improvements" that he had in mind. That year, however, there was a sudden disastrous fall in the price of black cattle, and the decline continued for the next three years. Allan and Flora went on with their plans for their children's future. Their eldest son Charles they managed to get into the East India service, with the help of Lady Margaret MacDonald and Mr. MacKenzie of Delvine. Lady Primrose, ever generous, outfitted him and paid for his passage.[4] Their elder daughter Anne was married in 1770 to Lieutenant Alexander MacLeod of Glendale.

Anne was sixteen; her husband, who was the illegitimate son of the chief of MacLeod, was a widower of forty or more. He was in the worldly sense a catch. Illegitimacy in the Highlands was no particular drawback; his father had acknowledged him and given him a tack in Vaternish, well stocked with cattle and horses, and made him factor of the MacLeod estates at a salary of seventy pounds a year, which was soon raised to a hundred pounds. He had inherited five hundred pounds from a half brother who had died in India, and he was a lieutenant of marines on half pay.

Although after Culloden the Highlanders had been forbidden to wear the Highland dress or to bear arms, when the Seven Years' War broke out and England needed men to fight against the French in America and elsewhere, Pitt, then Prime Minister, recruited 3,000 Highlanders, dressed them in tartan and sent them out, with their own chiefs and tacksmen for officers, to distinguish themselves fighting for King George. Alexander MacLeod had been with Wolfe at the siege of Quebec, had fought in India when the English took Pondicherry temporarily from the French, and in the Philippines when they had taken Manila, also temporarily, from the Spanish. He complained later that his health had been permanently impaired by those hot climates. When his regiment was "reduced" after the Peace of Paris in 1763, he had been retired on half pay and three years later had come home to Skye to take up the life of a tacksman.

It was said by Pennant that a tacksman of fifty pounds a year frequently employed twenty servants — and Alexander MacLeod had a good deal more money than that. He had also a well-stocked library, furniture, plate, horses, and the favor of the chief. He may have seemed a dazzling hero to sixteen-year-old Anne, and the marriage may have been by no means the rather distasteful affair of convenience that it appears at first sight. Alexander MacLeod showed himself throughout his life to be a vigorous, courageous, loyal, purposeful man of intelligence and discrimination — though apparently little more successful as a factor than Allan — and he and Anne seem to have been devoted to each other and to their four children.

In late July, 1772, the famous traveler Thomas Pennant visited Kingsburgh House. To his regret Flora herself was away on a visit, but he had a most satisfactory time with Allan, who put him in the very bed in which Prince Charles had slept and made him a present of the gloves that Charles had worn as Betty Burke. Kingsburgh also gave Pennant three "curious pieces of antiquity": an urn, a serpent bead and a denarius of the Emperor Trajan found not far from his house.[5] But he said nothing at all to his guest of that subject which was on all their minds — emigration.

9

Emigration Fever

FOR a good many years, even before Culloden, Scotsmen, and particularly Highlanders, had been seeking new homes and fortunes in America, especially in Nova Scotia, New York, Pennsylvania, Virginia, the Carolinas and Georgia. After 1763 the trickle swelled to a stream and then a flood, until, in 1775, the government becoming concerned about the loss of manpower, all emigration was prohibited. Estimates of the actual numbers of people who left Scotland between 1763 and 1775 range from ten to thirty thousand, but the consensus is that the really spectacular exodus was from the islands; four thousand are said to have left Skye alone. The numbers are not so interesting, however, as the reasons.

In December, 1773, the government, growing uneasy at the loss of so many artisans, farmers and potential soldiers and so much money — for many of the emigrants took substantial sums with them — required customs officials in the larger ports to register all emigrants: their names, ages, qualities, occupations, former residences and reasons for leaving the country. As most of the ships departed from smaller harbors or remote Highland lochs, these records represent only a sampling, but the reasons given for leaving are consistent: high rents, bad crops, loss of cattle, low wages, the high price of bread, unemployment, the hope of bettering their fortunes in the new country from which such good reports were coming. The enclosures and evictions, so tragic and well known, were to come later. It was for the most part poverty that drove the Scots out of Scotland in the years before the American Revolution, lured by reports of friends and family who had already gone to the land of plenty across the Atlantic, where food was abundant, land cheap, the soil rich, unemployment unknown, labor well paid and the climate favorable.

What especially distinguished this wave of emigration from later ones after the Revolution was the part that the tacksmen played in it. With the breakup of the clan system through the punitive measures after Culloden, the tacksmen's position changed and became more difficult. The chiefs, stripped of their power to administer justice and to raise their private armies, became primarily landowners, taking their rent in money instead of military services. Many of them had still a sense of responsibility for the members of their clans, but others wanted only to get as much money from the land as possible. The tacksmen's rents were drastically raised, some of them fourfold. As they were already squeezing all that was possible out of the peasants renting from them, they could not pass on the increase of rent but must manage somehow to pay it themselves. Some of the tacksmen went into the army; others, afraid of being sucked down into poverty and the peasantry, decided to emigrate while they still had money enough to establish themselves in a new land. Many of them took their tenants with them, some apparently hoping to re-establish the clan system, with themselves as chiefs, in the hills near Albany or the sand-pines region of North Carolina. The tenants, having been in the habit of following the tacksmen to war, now were ready to follow them across the seas, a state of mind which accounts in part for whole neighborhoods and whole glens emigrating in a body. The tacksmen also made some financial profit from the ship companies for enlisting passengers.

Many, perhaps most, of the emigrants went sadly. The Scotsman has always loved his land even though he left it, and he and his children and grandchildren look back on it with longing. "The laborers declare," says one customs house report, "they could not support their families on the wages they earned and that it is not from any other motive but the dread of want that they quit a country which above all others they would want to live in." When Dr. Johnson asked a Highlander if they, the Highlanders, would stay at home if they were well treated, he answered indignantly "that no man willingly left his native country."

In Skye it was the combination of serious losses of cattle, through bad weather and disease, and the greed of the new young chief that drove the MacDonalds away in great numbers in what Dr. Johnson called an "epidemic fury of emigration." MacLeod of MacLeod, who actually lowered his rents, kept the greater number of his tenants, and Raasay made so many wise concessions that he kept all of his people, but Sir Alexander of Sleat lost so many that the time was to come when he would have to bring into the island new tenants not of his own clan.

The unpopularity of the young Sir Alexander of Sleat seems to have been universal. He had been educated at Eton, where he was entered as Sandy MacDonald, and for seven years he was an ensign in the Coldstream Guards. He had married an English girl, a distant cousin of Boswell's, and for about five years they lived in Skye. When Johnson and Boswell visited them in 1773, they occupied a tenant's house in Armadale and were preparing to leave the island, for which they cared nothing, and move to Edinburgh. Bishop Forbes quotes a letter from an unnamed correspondent to Bishop Gordon dated May 9, 1771:

"2000 emigrants are preparing for their departure from the Isle of Skye to some part of our foreign settlements, perhaps the island of St. John [off the west coast of Newfoundland]. They are all of the estate of Sir Alexander who may chance to be a proprietor of land without tenants.

. . . All, *all* this is owing to the exorbitant rents from land."[1]

Old Kingsburgh, no longer able to write himself, dictated a letter to Mr. MacKenzie of Delvine in which he said, "Oh, since the late worthy Sir Alexʳ MacDonald and his amiable son Sir James are dead and gone, were either of them in being, the bearer, Mr. James MacDonald, would not be sent to London to freight vessels for about 500 passengers from this place to America."[2] This James MacDonald was the brother of Alexander MacDonald of Cuidreach, who had married Flora's half sister Annabella.

The spring of 1771, known as the Black Spring, was disastrous: so cold that snow lay on the ground for eight weeks; many cattle died, others had to be sold prematurely, and those that were left were emaciated. Emigration during this year drastically increased, and now for the first time the tide crept toward Flora. Her stepfather, Hugh of Armadale, and her sister Annabella and her family had all decided to go to North Carolina.

During that spring ten of the principal tacksmen on the Sleat estate held a meeting (opened by prayer) at which they resolved to "subscribe for a capital to purchase lands in America and settle a colony of their own," the minimum subscription to be twenty pounds.[3] The result of this meeting was a petition addressed to the King (who since 1761 had been George III) for 40,000 acres in North Carolina. Among those who signed were Alexander of Cuidreach and Hugh of Armadale.[4]

Annabella's husband, yet another Alexander MacDonald, was the fifth of his line to hold Cuidreach, one of the principal tacks of Sleat, not far from Kingsburgh, and he must have thought long and hard before he decided to leave it. When Marion MacDonald, Flora's mother, died is not known, but no doubt it was loneliness that made Hugh MacDonald decide to accompany his daughter and son-in-law to America.

North Carolina was probably selected because other Highlanders who had settled there had sent back glowing accounts. Three governors of the colony, first Governor Gabriel Johnson, himself a Scotsman, then Governors Tryon and Martin had done much to make settlement attractive to the Highlanders and to assist new arrivals there. A popular Gaelic song was widely sung: *Dod a ah'iarruidh an fhortain do North Carolina* — "Going to Seek a Fortune in North Carolina."

The petition for 40,000 acres was denied, but Cuidreach and Armadale decided to go anyhow. Annabella and her husband had five children, a son Donald and four younger girls. When they left, late in 1771 or early in 1772, Donald stayed behind, to join them later. Cuidreach's brothers James and Kenneth also followed after a year or two.

On February 13, 1772, old Kingsburgh died in his sleep. The honest, sturdy, loyal, kind old gentleman had been greatly loved. In the *Scots Magazine* there was a notice of his death:

"At Kingsburgh, in the 83rd year of his age, Alexander MacDonald of Kingsburgh. Our readers will remember this gentleman's hospitality to the Young Pretender in 1746, his bold avowal of what he had done, when in a situation that would have intimidated a man of less resolution."

By the following August, Flora and her husband had reached the decision to emigrate, although it would be two years more before they actually got off. On the twelfth of August Flora wrote to Mr. MacKenzie, who had promised to take the youngest boy, John, into his house to educate him:

Dr Sir

This goes by my Son Johnie who thank God tho I am misfortunat in other respects is happy in his haveing so good a freind as you are to take him under his protection, he seemed when here to be a good natured bidable Boy, without any kind of Vices, make of him what you please and may the Blessing of the almighty attend you along with him which is all the return I am able to make for your many and repeated freindships shown to me and this family; of which there will soon be no remembrance in this poor miserable Island, the best of its inhabitants are making ready to follow their freinds to America, while they have anything to bring there, and among the rest we are to go, especially as we cannot promise ourselves but poverty and oppression, haveing last Spring and this time two years lost almost our whole Stock of Cattle and horses; we lost within these three years, three hundred and twenty-seven heads, so that we have hardly what will pay our Creditors which we are to let them have and begin the world again, anewe, in anothere Corner of it. Allen was to write you but he is not well with a pain in his Side these ten days past. Sir I beg of you if you see anything amiss in the Boys conduct to let me know of it as some Children will stand in awe of their parents more than any body Else.

I am with my respects to you and Mrs. MacKenzie,

Sir with esteem

Your most obedient

humble servant

Flora mcdonald[5]

One might fear from this letter that Allan was suffering from an undiagnosed case of appendicitis but for the fact that Allan seems always to have faded out when there were letters to be written about the children. It was Flora who took responsibility for getting them started in life, as is evident from later letters. Her heavy heart, as she prepared to leave Skye and begin life anew in another corner of the world, is palpable.

The "good natured, bidable Johnie," who was thirteen years old at this time, had been at Edmund MacQueen's school at Portree. Two months later Flora sent a specimen of his handwriting to Mr. MacKenzie, and Mr. MacQueen wrote a covering letter to go with it, a letter which gives a vivid picture of the dominie himself. MacQueen wrote:

Though it is not such as I could wish, yet it is as good as can be expected from one of his age, considering the shortness of the time he has been at it particularly when it is but a by work being busy at the Latin—he reads Eutropius & gets the Grammer.

His genius is tolerably good with application suitable to his years. I am pretty well satisfied with the progress he has made. If you give any directions about him I shall follow them as far as I don't find them clash with the natural bent of his genius.[6]

Education through the Highlands at this time, as compared with other places, was remarkably widespread. Almost everyone could read,[7] and Johnson reported that in every house in the islands that he visited he found books in more than one language. One can see how this might be if all the schoolteachers were like Mr. MacQueen, strict yet surprisingly concerned for the natural bent of a child's "genius."

The sample of Johnny's handwriting can still be seen in the National Library of Scotland. It was brief. "Art has no enemy like an ignorant person," he wrote, twice, in a large copperplate hand, and added a somewhat cramped signature, John MacDonald.

It is not clear when it was that Alexander MacLeod and Anne decided to go to North Carolina too. In the same year, 1772, Alexander's father, Norman MacLeod, the twenty-second chief, died at St. Andrews and was succeeded by his grandson, Norman the twenty-third, his son John having died in India six years earlier. When the young chief came into possession of his estates he found them in a bad way. The old laird had gone deep into debt. Concessions had been made to the tenants to hold them; possibly Alexander Mac-Leod had been no more competent a factor than Allan MacDonald had been. The young Norman and his mother struggled to pull things together with the help of Alexander and also of the faithful MacKenzie of Delvine, but four years later he was to throw up the sponge, join the army, fight in

America and ultimately come home from India with the rank of major general.

Alexander's position suffered a change when his half nephew succeeded. He had already had some trouble with young Norman over a bond for a thousand pounds that the old chief, Alexander's father, had given him, to be paid for "services" after old Norman's death. A letter from Allan MacDonald, dated November 30, 1772, seeking Mr. Mac-Kenzie's help on behalf of his son-in-law, reveals that the young Norman had badgered the old gentleman until he signed a deed annulling the bond.[8] When the young chief succeeded, however, he evidently tried to do the fair thing, for in 1783 three different people testified that Alexander had been paid a hundred pounds by his nephew, possibly the best he could do with the estate in debt. Alexander nevertheless found it impossible to go on living in Skye. He resigned the factorship and in 1773 sold the stock on his farm for twelve hundred pounds and prepared to leave for North Carolina.

The emigration fever meanwhile had been mounting and spreading. Boswell took part in a dance that was invented to express the contagion of this fever. "They call it 'America,'" he wrote.

A brisk reel is played. The first couple begin, and each sets to one—then each to another—then as they set to the next couple, the second and third couples are setting; and so it goes on till all are set a-going, setting and wheeling round each other, while each is making the tour of all in the dance. It shows how emigration catches till all are set afloat. Mrs. Mackinnon told me that last year when the ship sailed from Portree for America, the people on shore were almost distracted when they saw their relations go off; they lay down on the ground and tumbled, and tore the grass with their teeth. This year there was not a tear shed. The people on shore seemed to think that they would soon follow. This is a mortal sign.[9]

❧ 10 ❧

Distinguished Visitors

IN September, 1773, two famous visitors came to Skye, the great Dr. Johnson and his friend Mr. Boswell. For many years, Boswell tells us, Dr. Johnson had given him hopes that they might go together and visit the Hebrides. The reason they gave for setting out on the three months' strenuous journey — the inveterate and usually ailing Londoner, whose prejudice against Scotland has been a standing joke for two centuries, and the young Scottish lawyer — was that they had read Martin's *Account of the Hebrides* and wished to "contemplate a system of life almost totally different from what we had been accustomed to see." Literary commentators have remarked also Boswell's desire to see his hero in a new and incongruous setting and enjoy the contrasts. Boswell himself, however, tactlessly told Sir Alexander Mac-Donald of Sleat that the real reason was to visit Flora Mac-Donald. When Boswell's book about the trip, *The Journal of a Tour to the Hebrides with Dr. Johnson,* was published, a year after Johnson's death, Sir Alexander wrote him furiously, "At your own behaviour every one felt some degree of resentment when you told me your only errand into Skye was to visit the Pretender's conductress, and that you deemed every moment as lost which was not spent in her company."[1]

It is possible that Boswell was only teasing Sir Alexander, for though he and Johnson were "both visibly of the *old interest,*" they were not exactly Jacobites. Both were Tories, but Johnson boggled at the divine right of kings and

Boswell "had high notions of male succession" and found that "Queen Mary [of Scots] comes in the way." Johnson furthermore explicitly said to Boswell that he "would not involve the nation in a civil war to restore the Stuarts. Nay, I have heard him say he was so dubious that if holding up his right hand would have gained the victory to the Highland army in 1745, he does not know if he would have done it. . . . With all this," Boswell summed it up, "he and I have a kind of *liking* for Jacobitism, something that it is not easy to define." In addition, Boswell the Lowlander had a sentiment about the Highlands that is shared by many romantics without even a tinge of Scottish blood. "The very Highland names," he said, "or the sound of a bagpipe, will stir my blood and fill me with a mixture of melancholy, and respect for courage; and pity for the unfortunate, and superstitious regard for antiquity; and inclination for war without thought; and, in short, with a crowd of sensations."

So the two set out, the "active, lively" Boswell, who had planned it all and got invitations for them from the chiefs of MacDonald and MacLeod, the formidable literary man, whose "person was large, robust, I may say approaching to the gigantic, and grown unwieldy from corpulency." The doctor wore "a full suit of plain brown clothes with twisted-hair buttons of the same colour, a large bushy greyish wig, a plain shirt, black worsted stockings, and silver buckles," and he carried in his pocket, for light reading, a volume called Ogden's *Sermons on Prayer*. He was in his sixty-fourth year; he had published his dictionary, written a novel — *Rasselas, the Prince of Abyssinia* — edited Shakespeare, and founded a club, to which Garrick, Reynolds, Burke, Goldsmith and others belonged and to which Boswell had recently been elected. The thirty-three-year-old Boswell, the son of Lord Auchinleck, a judge of the Court of Sessions in Scotland, was living at that time in James's Court, Edinburgh, with his sweet dull wife and his infant daughter Veronica — and running away to London as often as he could manage it.

Johnson went to Edinburgh to join Boswell for the trip. From there they traveled by coach to Inverness; north of Inverness, where there were no roads to speak of, they went on horseback, with two Highlanders to run alongside and lead the horses. They had with them also an extra horse for the baggage and Boswell's manservant, Joseph Ritter, a tall, fine-looking Hungarian.

Fifteen days after leaving Edinburgh they reached Armadale, where they visited Sir Alexander and Lady Mac-Donald. Here they found everything mean and unsuitable, though the situation of the house among its trees, with a little brook running downhill beside it, was attractive enough. But the dinner was ill-dressed, there was no claret and no wheat loaf; at tea they had to use their fingers for the sugar. Lady MacDonald, though in her twenties and considered beautiful, was to Johnson dull and heavy. Still, there was a piper at breakfast and dinner, and one night there was muirfowl for supper, which comforted Boswell somewhat, though he put Sir Alexander in a passion by taking him to task for his parsimony. It must be said for Sir Alexander that he and his lady were already packing up to move to Edinburgh. A month later they were gone.

After staying four days at Armadale they went off on horses borrowed from Sir Alexander to visit the MacKinnons at Coirechatachan, a farm which Lachlan MacKinnon rented from his chief. Mrs. MacKinnon was old Kingsburgh's daughter, Allan's sister, who had been Mrs. MacAllister when the Prince spent the night at Kingsburgh House. She was, according to Boswell, "a decent, well-behaved old gentlewoman in a black silk gown." Boswell and Johnson found everything at Coirechatachan in good condition: a carpet on the parlor floor, as there had not been at Armadale; a silver tea service, with tongs. For supper they had a large dish of minced beef collops, a large dish of fricassee of fowl, friar's chicken, a dish of ham or tongue, some excellent haddocks, a large bowl of rich milk, frothed, as good a bread pudding as Boswell had ever tasted, full of raisins and lemon or orange peel, and sillabubs made with port wine and in sillabub glasses. There was a good tablecloth with napkins, china, silver spoons and, to drink, porter and a large bowl of very good punch. Dr. Johnson, as usual, drank tea or lemonade.

Mrs. MacKinnon reminisced about that famous night at Kingsburgh House; she also was capable of properly admiring Dr. Johnson, in which Lady MacDonald no doubt had failed.

Five delightful days at Raasay followed, where they met Malcolm MacLeod, now a man of sixty-two, "quite the Highland gentleman: of a stout well-made person, well-proportioned; a manly countenance browned with the weather, but a ruddiness in his cheeks, a good way up which his rough beard extended; a quick lively eye, not fierce in his look, but firm and good-humoured." Malcolm also regaled the visitors with accounts of his experiences with the Prince and of his capture and imprisonment on the *Furnace*, ending with what must have become a formula after all these years, "So I went to London to be hanged, and came down in a chaise with Miss Flora MacDonald." They had a very gay time at Raasay, with a large company that included the chief's ten daughters and three sons and dancing at night. "Raarsa himself danced with his children," Dr. Johnson wrote to Mrs. Thrale, "and old Malcolm in his Fillibeg [kilt] was as nimble as when he led the prince over the mountains."

They came to Kingsburgh House on September twelfth and spent the night there. Allan was out to welcome them and to lead Dr. Johnson into the house. Like Malcolm MacLeod, he was the very picture of a gallant Highlander.

He had his tartan plaid thrown about him, a large blue bonnet
with a knot of black ribbon like a cockade, a brown short coat of
a kind of duffle, a tartan vest with gold buttons and gold button-
holes, a bluish filibeg, and tartan hose. He had jet-black hair tied
behind and with screwed ringlets on each side, and was a large
stately man, with a steady sensible countenance.

The Highland dress was still forbidden by law and according to Dr. Johnson very little used. Sir Alexander wore
the tartan, but he of course was a chief. Malcolm MacLeod's
kilt was purple and Allan's bluish.

Allan led his guests into the parlor, where a good fire was
burning, and offered them Holland gin. Flora did not appear
until supper was brought in.

"She was a little woman," wrote Boswell, "of a mild and
genteel appearance, mighty soft and well bred. To see Mr.
Samuel Johnson salute Miss Flora MacDonald was a won-
derful romantic scene to me."[2]

Flora had first heard about the impending visit about
two weeks earlier when she was staying on the mainland
with friends. "I heard," she told Johnson archly, "that Mr.
Boswell was coming to Skye, and one Mr. Johnson, a young
English buck, with him." Johnson was delighted with this
and referred to himself afterwards as a buck.

Johnson too said that he "saluted" Flora, and they undoubtedly meant that he kissed her.

"I had the honor of saluting the far famed Miss Flora
MacDonald," he wrote Mrs. Thrale,

who conducted the Prince dressed as her Maid through the
English forces from the Island of Lewes and when she came to
Skie, dined with the English officers and left her Maid below.
She must then have been a young Lady, she is not now old, of a
pleasing person and elegant behavior. She told me that she
thought herself honored by my visit and I am sure that whatever

regard she bestowed on me was liberally repaid. "If thou likest her opinions thou wilt praise her virtue." She was carried to London but dismissed without a trial, and came down with Malcolm MacLeod, against whom sufficient evidence could not be procured. She and her husband are poor, and are going to try their fortune in America.[3]

The wife of Allan's brother James was there for supper, and one of the MacDonalds' sons. Supper at Kingsburgh House — it is a relief to learn — was as genteel as anyone could wish, with an excellent roasted turkey, porter to drink at table, and after supper claret and punch. "But what I admired," said Boswell, "was the perfect ease with which everything went on."

Johnson was coming down with a cold and he went to bed early, but Boswell sat up with Kingsburgh and his brother and Mr. MacQueen, the minister, and among them they drank three bowls of the "superexcellent" punch.

The room that Boswell and Johnson shared was the room in which the Prince had slept, and Johnson had the bed itself, though not the sheets, which had been buried with Mrs. MacDonald as she had desired. Both beds had tartan curtains, and the room was decorated with maps and prints, including Hogarth's print of John Wilkes with the cap of liberty beside him. Boswell savored the scene to the utmost.

"To see Mr. Samuel Johnson," he wrote, "lying in Prince Charles's bed, in the Isle of Skye, in the house of Miss Flora Macdonald, struck me with such a group of ideas as it is not easy for words to describe as the mind perceives them. He smiled, and said, 'I have had no ambitious thoughts in it.'"

On the table in the room Dr. Johnson left a slip of paper on which he had written, "Quantum cedat virtutibus aurum," which Boswell translated, "With virtue weigh'd, what worthless trash is gold!"

At breakfast Johnson spoke of his pleasure in having

slept in the bed. Boswell said that he was the lucky man and that it had been contrived between Mrs. MacDonald and him.

"She said, 'You know young *bucks* are always favourites of the ladies.' He spoke of the Prince being here, and said to Mrs. MacDonald, '*Who* was with him? We were told in England, there was one Miss Flora Macdonald with him.' Said she, 'They were very right.' "

She then told them the whole story, of the costume, the crossing, the coming to Mugstot, and how she had dined with the officer who was looking for the Prince and laughed at him often afterwards for having deceived him.

When the visitors left Kingsburgh House, Dr. Johnson suffering from his cold and a little deaf, Kingsburgh took them in his boat across Loch Snizort to a place a mile beyond Greshornish, where the horses had been sent ahead to meet them. This set them on their way to Dunvegan with a saving of eight miles of hard riding. Dr. Johnson thought riding in Skye very unpleasant, for the roads were narrow and rough; one could enjoy neither conversation nor contemplation.

It was nearly two months more before Johnson and Boswell were back in Edinburgh, after many adventures, much good conversation and some interesting reflections on the Highlands. Two years later Johnson published his book in the trip, *A Journey to the Western Isles of Scotland,* in which he said that the name of Flora MacDonald would be "mentioned in history, and if courage and fidelity be virtues, mentioned with honor. She is a woman of middle stature, soft features, gentle manners and elegant presence."[4]

Ten years after that, when Dr. Johnson had been dead nearly a year, Boswell made the diary that he had kept faithfully on the trip into the famous *Journal of a Tour to the Hebrides,* which, even though bowdlerized by his friend Edmond Malone, was so indiscreet that it evoked a good deal of criticism and enraged Sir Alexander MacDonald to the point of writing Boswell a long and abusive letter about it. A duel was mentioned but came to nothing.

There was nothing more in the book than what has already been quoted about Flora or her husband, except for one romantic thought that Boswell had as they were crossing Loch Snizort: "While I sailed in Kingsburgh's boat and thought of the emigration, it did not hurt me. I fancied him sailing in America just as he did about Skye."

11

Going to Seek a Fortune in North Carolina

IN the time that remained before Flora and Allan left for
North Carolina, they wound up their affairs in Skye, packed
the possessions that they would take with them and arranged, so far as they could, to settle their children on a
course of life.

Charles, the eldest, now twenty-three, was safe in the
East India Company. Twenty-year-old Anne, with her husband Alexander MacLeod and their two little boys, was
preparing to leave at the same time, if not on the same boat,
as Flora and Allan. Tradition says the two families traveled
together, but there is nothing to substantiate it.

Ranald at seventeen was a lieutenant in the marines,
through the good offices of Captain Charles Douglas of the
Ardent ship-of-war, who had some pull with the Admiralty.
Captain Douglas has not heretofore appeared in the story of
Flora's life and will not again, but it is possible that he had
been one of the several young men on the *Bridgewater* or
the *Eltham* who became such staunch friends of hers.

Fifteen-year-old John had already been for two years
with the MacKenzies of Delvine, attending school in Edinburgh and making good use of his time.

Alexander, eighteen, James, seventeen, and Fanny, the
youngest, who was only eight, were still be to be settled.

It was Flora rather than Allan who was concerned about
Alexander. As a desperate measure she decided to appeal to
the Duke of Atholl for help in launching him. This Duke was
the nephew of the one who died in the Tower of London in

July, 1746, a prisoner for his part in the 'Forty-five. Flora did not know him personally but she evidently thought that he might feel some kindness for her because of her contribution to the Jacobite cause. After trying in vain to induce Allan to write to him, she engaged Alexander as amanuensis and dictated a letter dated 23 April, 1774 — either to show off her son's proficiency in penmanship or to disguise her own deficiency, which seems to have persisted in spite of Mr. Beatt's efforts.

My Lord

Necessity often forces both sexes to go through many transactions contrary to their inclinations. Such is the present one as nothing but real necessity could force me to give your Grace this trouble, & open my miserable state to your Lordship's view with the hope of getting some comfort through your wonted goodness of heart to many who have been in less tribulation of mind than I am at present.

The case is as follows — my husband by various losses & the education of our children (having no other legacy to leave them) fell through the little means we had, so as not to be able to keep this possession, especially as the rents are so prodigiously augmented; therefore of course must contrary to our inclination follow the rest of our friends who have gone this three years passed to America; but before I go would wish to have one or two boys I have still unprovided for in some shape or other off my hands. The oldest of the two called Alexander is bordering on nineteen years of age, hath a pretty good handwriting, as this letter may attest, went through the most of the classicks & the common rules of Arithmetick, so that he is fit for whatever providence and the recommendation of well wishers may throw in his way; your Grace's doing something for him would be the giving of real relief to my perplexed mind before I leave (with reluctance) my native land & a real piece of charity.

After telling of the settling of Charles, Ranald and John, she returned to Alexander.

Had I this boy off my hands before I leave the Kingdom I could almost leave it with pleasure, even tho' I have a Boy and a lassie still depending on the protection of kind providence.

This freedom I am hope full your Grace will forgive as nothing but the care of my family could prevail with me to use such.

Mr. Macdonald though he once had the honour of a little of your Grace's acquaintance could not be prevailed upon to put pen to paper therefore I with the assistance of what remained of the old resolution, went through this bold task. And with the prayers of a poor distressed woman (once known to the world) for the prosperity of your family

I am, with the greatest esteem & respect
Yr. Grace's most obedient Servant
Flora mcdonald[1]

It is this letter, no doubt, that has given rise to a fairly general feeling that Allan MacDonald was rather a poor creature who, unsuccessful as a factor and a farmer, dragged his wife to America, leaving it to her to provide for their son. But Allan may have regarded the appeal to the Duke of Atholl as presumptuous and unlikely to succeed; he may well have felt that the boys would do better to go with their parents to America and make their fortunes there. Though he was never successful financially, the times were against him, and other able men fared as badly as he did. He showed himself throughout to be a man of courage, resolution and loyalty, hard pressed but conscientious. What comes through the letter in almost every sentence is Flora's grief over leaving Skye, her distrust of the venture, her troubled acquiescence in it.

Nothing came of the letter. They decided to take Alexander and James with them but to leave Fanny behind in the care of friends. It is not known which friends, but it seems probable that it was the MacLeods of Raasay, for when Flora returned from America, more than five years later, she went to Raasay to get Fanny.

The family there would be a good one with which to leave a little girl. There were ten daughters — Flora, Janet, Katherine, Margaret, Isabella, Jane, Julia, Anne, Mary and Christian — and three sons, and Dr. Johnson himself said that they were the best-bred children he ever saw. It was a warm, happy, hospitable, fun-loving household. They entertained lavishly in their large new house, danced every night, had quantities of good food and never suffered from toothache. All ten girls, in spite of Dr. Johnson's fears for them in their remote out-of-the-world home, eventually made good marriages.

The packing up of the MacDonalds' possessions — plate, books and furniture valued at five hundred pounds — and getting them to the boat must, in those days when moving vans were nonexistent and the roads no more than tracks, have been a formidable undertaking. When they left Kingsburgh, the tack was taken over by a MacLeod of Ose, who kept it until 1790.[2]

There is a firm tradition which says that they sailed from Campbeltown in Kintyre on the *Bristol* and arrived in the port of Brunswick, North Carolina, in August, 1774. Campbeltown was near Largie; it would have been natural and convenient to stay with the MacDonald cousins before they left the country. Elizabeth, Flora's contemporary and second cousin, had succeeded to the estate, the fourteenth of her line to hold it; she had married Mr. Charles Lockhart, who changed his name to MacDonald, in order to keep the name going at Largie into the fourteenth generation.

That they sailed in the summer of 1774 we know from the Loyalist Papers, but the name of their ship is not given there. The Brunswick Port of Entry Book, though the records for some years are mutilated, is clear and complete for the latter half of 1774 — and there is no mention in it of the *Bristol*. In August thirteen vessels came in, bringing ballast, puncheons, rum, sugar and Negroes. On October 18, the

Ulysses, a ship of 115 tons, bonded at Greenock, docked with a cargo of linen, shoes, sugar, thirty-two-dozen hats, woolens, sailcloth, gunpowder, pewter, earthenware, mustard, linseed oil, paint, glass, silks, port wine and 111 Scottish passengers, who might conceivably have included Flora and her family.

But whatever ship it was that brought Flora and Allan, Alexander and James and eight indentured servants (five men, three women), it was probably very like other ships of the time of which we have descriptions: incredibly small by today's standards, square-sailed, with fairly comfortable accommodations for the gentry and miserable quarters for the common folk.

When Boswell and Johnson passed through Portree on their way from Raasay to Kingsburgh, they saw the *Nestor* lying in the harbor waiting to pick up emigrants, and Boswell with his insatiable curiosity went aboard.

The cabin was commodious and even elegant. There was a little library, finely bound. I looked at nothing except a volume of the Rev. Mr. Hervey's works lying on the table. The accommodation for the emigrants was very good. A long ward I may call it, with a row of beds on each side, every one of which was the same size every way, and fit to contain four people.[3]

Boswell took the plight of the middle two in those square beds very lightly, but Janet Schaw, a charming and witty woman of about Flora's age, who sailed from Edinburgh to North Carolina that same year, looked upon the emigrants in a similar situation with horrified compassion. She herself and the young girl traveling with her had a narrow stateroom, with Miss Schaw's maid sleeping on the floor between their bunks, while her brother and two small boys of the party slept in the main cabin. The wretched passengers in the stinking dormitory between the decks subsisted on a small allowance of oatmeal, potatoes, neck beef and spoilt pork. To feed the gentry there were pigs, sheep, chickens and ducks in coops on the deck, as well as barrels of flour, onions, kegs of butter and other luxuries. That these were all washed away in a storm and the company thereafter ate lobscourse, stirabout and scratch-platter was an accidental part of the voyage and probably not an uncommon one.[4]

In any case the crossing took from six weeks to two months, and the passengers were undoubtedly thankful when they smelled land at last and heard the waves booming on the Frying Pan Shoals at the mouth of the Cape Fear River.

12

The New Home

TO Janet Schaw, who came soon after Flora, the first sight of North Carolina was dismal. "A dreary waste of white barren sand and melancholy nodding pines," she wrote in her journal letter to a friend in Edinburgh. "My heart dies within me, while I view it." Those whose eyes were accustomed to Skye's misty mountains and deep-cut sealochs must have felt their hearts, too, die within them.

They came first to Fort Johnston on the west bank of the Cape Fear River, a small, squat, harmless rampart built of tapia, a concoction of lime, sand, oyster shells and water poured into box forms and hardened, not unlike present-day cinder blocks. Here the incoming ship must stop, present its credentials to the captain of the fort and pay a fee. Riding at anchor nearby was an old sloop of war, the *Cruizer*, which the passengers may or may not have noticed but which they would hear much about later.

Twelve miles above the mouth of the river, on comparatively high ground, also on the western bank, was Brunswick, the port of entry and clearance. Miss Schaw found it "very poor — a few scattered houses on the edge of the woods, without street or regularity." Streets it did have, though an Edinburgh lady might not recognize them as such. Front Street and Second Street ran parallel to the river and others were laid out to intersect them at right angles. There was at least one public house, Roger's Tavern, consisting of six rooms, each with its fireplace faced with Delft tiles and its door opening onto the yard; there were also a

135

church, a customs house, a courthouse, a jail, some stores and some dwelling houses, more than fifty buildings altogether. To the north and south of the town were plantations: Russellboro, where Governor Tryon had lived for a time, and York, the home of the Moore family, who had fifty years earlier laid out the town as a real estate venture.

The "better sort" of traveler did not stay at inns but were entertained as a matter of course by planters or rich merchants. If the MacDonalds disembarked at Brunswick, they possibly spent the night at William Dry's house, which Josiah Quincy of Massachusetts, who had been there the year before, called "the house of universal hospitality." Mr. Dry, the collector of customs, was a Whig. "He talks treason by the hour," said Miss Schaw disdainfully. Or if they stayed with the Moores of York, there too they would have quickly been made aware of the stirrings of discontent in the province, for the Moore family were already actively Whig in their sympathies.

They may, however, have gone on twenty miles farther to Wilmington, the flourishing town on the eastern side of the river at the point where its northeast and northwest branches diverged. With a better harbor, less exposed to storms and pirates, closer to the back country and its supplies, Wilmington was growing as Brunswick declined. Here their hosts would be Lowland Scots merchants staunchly loyal to the King. From them too they might learn that at New Bern, where Governor Josiah Martin lived in the "palace" built by his predecessor Tryon, a provincial congress had met at the end of August in open defiance of the Governor and that it had elected three representatives to a continental congress which in October was sitting in Philadelphia.

Tradition says that when Flora MacDonald landed in North Carolina she was joyously welcomed by her fellow countrymen already there with parades and parties and that

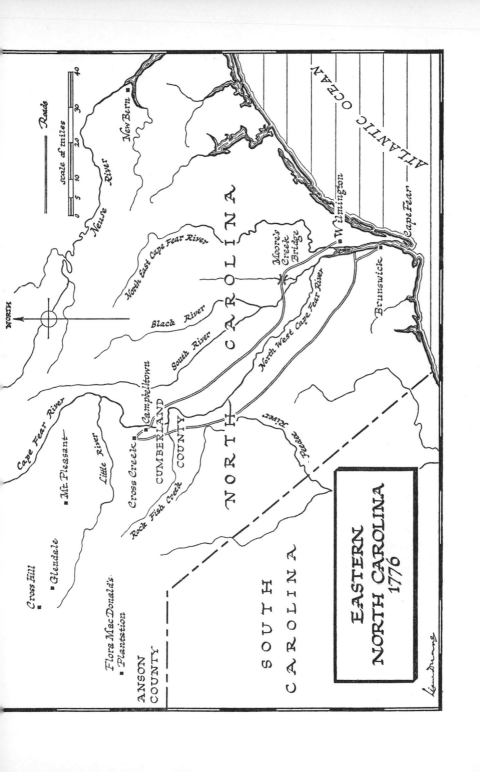

EASTERN
NORTH CAROLINA
1776

in Wilmington a great ball was given in her honor, at which, according to J. P. MacLean, the author of *Flora MacDonald in America,* "she was greatly gratified by the special attention bestowed on her daughter Anne, then entering into womanhood and of surpassing beauty."[1] Anne at this time had been married three years and was the mother of two children, possibly pregnant with her third; there is furthermore no record of such a ball, no echo of it in Janet Schaw's journal. It is much more likely that the MacDonald family arrived quietly and very soon made their way, either by boat or by road to the Highland settlements in the sand-hill country on the upper reaches of the northwest branch of the Cape Fear River. The back country attracted them, not only because other Highlanders had already settled there but also because various manuals for emigrants published in Scotland had described it as being higher, healthier, more productive land than the flat, mosquito-and-hurricane-ridden tidal regions along the coast.

If they went by boat it would have taken them approximately a week to cover the ninety miles, rowing against the current at a rate of fourteen miles a day. The river was a busy stream of commerce, with flatboats and lighters and pirogues carrying grain, lumber and barrels of salted meat to the coast and bringing back needles and hats and rum and sugar and other salable items to the stores in Cross Creek and Campbelltown. Now and then there might be a smart boat from one of the plantations near Wilmington, with an awning to keep off the sun and six Negro slaves in neat uniforms to row it, but for the most part they were working craft that plied the river.

If the travelers took the road that followed along the west side of the river through the moss-hung forest, they would go on horseback. Possibly some friendly planter might have lent or rented them a phaeton and four for the ladies and the small children; if so, it was a luxury they would not enjoy again. In the back country, even among the well-to-do, carriages were rare. None were listed in the inventories of the MacDonalds or the MacLeods, though wagons were. Everybody, however, had horses. "A man must be very poor," said Janet Schaw's brother Alexander, "who walks on foot."[2] Flora, who came from a part of Scotland where there were no roads for carriages, would take riding as a matter of course. Along the way they might meet wagons loaded with grain or drovers with herds of black cattle heading toward Wilmington.

Whichever way they went, by road or by water, it must have been beautiful. Even Miss Schaw, after she recovered from her first sight of sand and pines, conceded that. "Nothing," she wrote, "can be finer than the banks of this river; a thousand beauties both of the flowery and sylvan tribe hang over it and are reflected from it with additional lustre." William Bartram the botanist, who went by road from Wilmington to Cross Creek in 1777, was equally enthusiastic and more knowledgeable; he gave the Latin names for all the variety of trees and shrubs and wildflowers along the way, and a geological analysis of the soil as well.

The North Carolina coastal plain spread of more than a hundred miles inland from the sea. The soil was a light, sandy loam, productive where it was cleared and fertile along the rivers and creeks. The planters in the lower Cape Fear region raised indigo, rice, corn and wheat, though not enough of the last even for their own needs. Their chief source of wealth was the miles of pine forest from which they took the naval stores, the pitch and tar and turpentine, the lumber and the shingles, which they shipped to England and to the West Indies. In the pine-covered sand hills and rich creek valleys of the upper Cape Fear, people raised black cattle, horses, hogs and grain, which they sent overland to Charles Town in South Carolina or down the river to Wilmington. They did not tap the trees for turpentine, for

139

that was tedious work best performed by slaves, and few of the Scotsmen of the sand hills owned slaves, though they made use of indentured servants.

Cross Creek and Campbelltown at the head of navigation on the Cape Fear were twin villages a mile and three quarters apart. Campbelltown stood on the flat and swampy land on the river itself, Cross Creek on a bluff over the creek for which it was named, at the beginning of the sand hills which rolled away to the west behind it. In 1778 the two villages were combined into one under the name Campbelltown and five years later were renamed Fayetteville, the first town in America thus to honor Lafayette. In 1774, when the MacDonalds arrived, both were thriving trade centers with mills, shops, dwelling houses, a pharmacy and a courthouse, thronged with people and with wagons from the back country laden with goods to be sent to the coast by road or river.

The first Scottish settlers in the upper Cape Fear had come in 1732, a mere trickle. They were followed by a steady stream, until by 1754 the region was populated thickly enough for the provincial legislature to create a new county, which it named Cumberland, a strange name to give to a home for Highland Scots only eight years after Culloden, even though many of them had come from Argyll, which had been loyal to the government. The Highlanders continued to pour into the country in waves which reached a crest in 1774 and 1775, when there were, it has been estimated, about ten thousand of them in the region. They made up, however, only about half of the population of Cumberland County; the rest were English, Irish, Welsh, German, Lowland Scots and a few French.

Some of the Highlanders were artisans, but most of them came with a hunger for land, eager to establish themselves as planters and landlords. Some, especially among the earlier arrivals, took up land grants; others who had more money bought already established farms on which they raised black cattle as they had done in Scotland. The former tacksmen lived much as they had lived at home, but the small farmers found life considerably richer and easier here. They raised corn and hogs for their staple food; fished in the rivers and creeks; shot deer, wild turkeys, pheasant, quail, ducks, wild geese and wild pigeons, with no complaint from anyone about poaching; and got just for the picking all the wild grapes, strawberries, blackberries, apples, mulberries, cherries and persimmons that they could eat. The former crofters who had subsisted on oatmeal and milk must have felt themselves in clover.

Flora and her family went first to Cross Creek but did not linger there. Annabella and Alexander MacDonald of Cuidreach, who had already been in North Carolina for nearly three years, were waiting for them at Mt. Pleasant, about twenty-five miles farther west, and they pushed on.

What was then Mt. Pleasant in Cumberland County is now Cameron's Hill in Harnett. On the south side of an elevation about six hundred feet high was the plantation of two hundred acres which Alexander of Cuidrech had bought in 1772. In the short time that he had had it, he had increased the cleared and cultivated land from thirty to forty-five acres, added rooms to the dwelling house, planted orchards of peach and apple, acquired cattle, horses and hogs. He had been appointed a justice of the peace by the Governor. Here he and Annabella, who were in their early forties, lived with their four daughters Their eldest child and only son Donald came from Scotland at Christmas time in this same year of 1774 to join them. Alexander's younger brothers, James and Kenneth, had also settled in Cumberland, and Hugh MacDonald of Armadale had two plantations in Anson County, fifty miles to the west.[3]

The house at Mt. Pleasant was probably built of squared logs covered with wood siding, unpainted, and provided with chimneys at each end. The kitchen and servants' quarters would be separate buildings, also of logs. Dr. Murdoch MacLeod, the surgeon of Cross Creek and himself the owner of farms in Anson and Cumberland counties, said that Cuidreach's house was well furnished. They had brought with them from Skye silver teaspoons, knives and forks, silver salt cellars and a complete tea equipage, chairs and chests and beds, twenty pairs of blankets, ten pairs of sheets, half a dozen tablecloths. Their sixty volumes of books were on shelves around the walls. Another friend, Major MacLean, declared that the house was "very decently furnished" and that the situation was "delightful."

After the long ocean voyage, the possibly disappointing and distressing arrival, the more than a hundred miles' trek into the back country, it must have been immensely reassuring to Flora and Allan MacDonald to come to this hospitable house, to see firelight on silver and books and polished wood, and to hear the news of the other members of the family who had come to America before them. They settled down to spend a few weeks, or perhaps even months, here, while Allan and his sons made trips into the sand hills to find a suitable place for them to buy.

Near the house at Mt. Pleasant was a spring of clear water rising through the sandy ground under a canopy of trees, which is still known in the neighborhood as Flora MacDonald's spring. People say that she used to sit here, dreaming and smoking her pipe, while she waited for Allan to return with the news that he had found a home for them.

About a mile away on Barbecue Creek was Barbecue Church, built in 1765 or 1766, where first the Reverend James Campbell and then John MacLeod came to preach in Gaelic and in English. Unquestionably while she was at Mt. Pleasant Flora attended services at this church. Henry Foote, writing in 1847, told of meeting an old lady, a Mrs. Smith, who remembered in her childhood seeing Flora

MacDonald at Barbecue Church, "a dignified and handsome woman to whom all paid respect" and "always womanly in her course and always lovely."[4]

A modern red-brick church stands there now near the site of the first one. In the graveyard, which is full of Cameron headstones, with a Campbell or two in the corners, there is a touching early grave which shows how those first Highland settlers felt about the hills which they had left. It is the grave of a six-months-old boy, whose body was carried here on horseback by his twelve-year-old brother because the family, who lived some miles away in the direction of the coast, wanted to bury their child on a hill, and the only hill available was this six-hundred-foot Mt. Pleasant.

Anson County, to the west and south of Cumberland, was a region of sandy soil, low hills, forests of longleaf pine, swamps grown with canebrake, winding creeks bordered with oak, elm and tulip trees, with a ground cover of pea vine on which the cattle throve and which has since disappeared. Many of the Highlanders had settled in Anson, including Murdoch MacLeod the surgeon and Flora's stepfather Hugh; Cuidreach had a second plantation here.

Allan bought from one Caleb Touchstone 475 acres in Anson (now Montgomery) County, with seventy acres cleared and in cultivation and three good orchards of peach, apple and other fruits. There were already a gristmill on a good run of water (probably Cheek's Creek), a dwelling house, kitchen, barn, stable, keeping house and crib for Indian corn. He bought too a smaller farm of fifty acres of which thirty were in cultivation, also with its dwelling houses and outhouses.

To his plantation on Cheek's Creek he brought his wife, his sons Alexander and James, his eight indentured servants, and the books, plate and furniture from Kingsburgh House. According to tradition, he named the new home Killiegray, but in this tradition errs. There was an island named

Killegray in the Sound of Harris between Harris and North Uist, but it was MacLeod country and there was no reason why Flora and Allan should have chosen that name for their new home. The North Carolina antiquaries who have made a lifetime study of these settlements agree that Killiegray was the name of a plantation owned by a Captain Alexander MacLeod who is often and understandably confused with Flora's son-in-law.

Anne and Alexander MacLeod also found their home that winter, about twenty-five miles from Mt. Pleasant in Cumberland County (now Moore), a little south of the present town of Carthage. Though Alexander MacLeod bought land adjoining Cuidreach's in Anson County, he did not live on it; the land on which he lived, and which he farmed, he did not own. He rented it from Kenneth Black, the son of Malcolm Black of Jura, who had come to North Carolina in 1740.

Alexander and Anne gave the name of Glendale to their home, and they lived there as long as they were in North Carolina. Alexander's library, which was large for the time and scholarly, gives some indication of the man and his interests. He made a complete inventory of it later for the Loyalist Claims Commission. The 324 volumes — 129 titles — included history, philosophy, poetry, drama, religion, a biographical dictionary in eleven volumes, recent novels such as *Tom Jones, Joseph Andrews* and *Robinson Crusoe,* some books on husbandry, *The Scots Peerage,* and bound volumes of the *Scots Magazine.* He had dozens of silver knives, forks and spoons, twenty-seven pairs of fine new blankets, an embroidered satin bedcover which the Rebels would sell later for thirty pounds at a vendue, looking glasses, china, earthenware and stoneware, his own wearing apparel (valued at eighty pounds) and Anne's (valued at one hundred and twenty pounds), forty-one tablecloths, old and new. He soon acquired a stock of cattle, horses and hogs.

They had twelve indentured servants. Here at Glendale during the next two years two more children were to be born.[5]

Flora and her daughter and her half sister were now scattered through the sand hills, Flora fifty miles away from Annabella, about twenty-five from Anne. Her stepfather, Hugh, was nearest to her, five miles or so away on Cheek's Creek. Later Hugh would make 200 of his acres over to Donald, Annabella's son, and give 200 more to Cuildreach to add to the land that he already owned there. The Highland settlers, as fast as they could manage it, were increasing their holdings, renting out what they did not use themselves, evidently with the idea of repeating in the new country the pattern that they most admired in the old, the large landed estate with many tenants.

Exactly when Flora and Allan moved to Anson County is not known. The Committee of Safety in Wilmington, deciding on July 3, 1775, to write to Allan, believed him to be living in Cumberland County, but the Committee of Safety did not necessarily have accurate information as to his whereabouts. In April, 1776, the Provincial Congress knew him as a resident of Anson, though by that time he had left there. It seems likely that Flora and Allan with their two sons and eight servants would wish to make their visit to Annabella and Alexander as brief as possible and that they would be still more eager to get started on their new life as early as they could. Flora herself said that they lived "comfortably" on the plantation in Anson for nearly a year. It is reasonable to assume that they moved to Anson County in the spring of 1775.

What is certain is that they were immediately involved in what Allan called "the Troubles," the beginning of the American Revolution.

🌸 13 🌸

The Highlanders Take Sides

ALLAN MacDonald had a cousin of about his own age who was then living in Staten Island, New York. Captain Alexander MacDonald, having served in the 'Forty-five in one of the independent companies of Sir Alexander MacDonald of Sleat, had stayed on in the army and fought in the French and Indian War both on the American continent and in the West Indies. After his regiment was "reduced" in 1763, he remained in New York, began to speculate in land and married Susan Meyer, whose mother was a Livingston. Ten years later they bought a farm on Staten Island, where with their four children they were living when the Troubles began.

Though the Livingstons were notable Whigs, Alexander and his wife were convinced Loyalists. In the winter of 1775 Alexander went from Staten Island to the Highland settlements on the Mohawk River and enlisted a company of 200 Highlanders to fight for the King. On his return he sent an officer disguised as a peddler to North Carolina to inform the Highlanders there of what was going on in New York.[1]

A number of the Captain's letters to Allan during the years 1777 to 1779 have survived, but unfortunately there is none that was written to him during 1775 and 1776. It is likely that they were in communication then too and that when this officer in the guise of a peddler reached the Highland settlements in Anson and Cumberland counties, he sought out Allan MacDonald.

The tension between Britain and the American colonies

146

was fast gathering strength and heat. In May, 1774, General Thomas Gage had arrived in Boston and closed the port under the Coercive Acts as punishment for the Boston Tea Party of the previous December. The first Continental Congress, held in Philadelphia in September and October, 1774, while reasserting its loyalty to the King, had advised the colonies to form their own militia, adopted a nonimportation and nonexportation agreement and recommended the establishment of Committees of Safety throughout the colonies.

In Massachusetts during the winter of 1775 the new militia was drilling, selected companies of "minutemen" held themselves ready to respond on a minute's notice, and supplies of arms and ammunition were being collected and stored at Concord. In Virginia on March 13 Patrick Henry cried out, "Give me liberty or give me death!" In North Carolina the Wilmington Committee of Safety met eighty-four times between November 23, 1774, and March 7, 1776.[2]

The Royal Governor of North Carolina, Josiah Martin, was a man of thirty-seven, who had been born in Antigua, one of the twenty-three children of the popular Colonel Samuel Martin. He spent fifteen years in the British army before he retired in 1769, on the grounds of ill health, and sold his commission. A loyal and impulsive man of little judgment, he set about meeting the crisis in North Carolina with a deficiency of understanding of the people, an over-supply of self-confidence and a total lack of effective assistance from England. On the first of March, 1775, he issued the first of four proclamations calling for loyalty to the King, on the sixteenth he wrote to General Gage in Boston that he could raise 3,000 Regulators and a considerable body of Highlanders and asked for arms and ammunition — a letter which was intercepted by the Colonists — and early in April he summoned a meeting of the Assembly (the colonial legislature) and forbade the meeting of a special provincial congress called by the Whigs to elect delegates to the

Second Continental Congress, to be held in Philadelphia in May.

Both groups, the legal Assembly and the illegal Congress, proceeded to meet in New Bern. The membership of both was substantially the same. The Speaker of the Assembly, John Harvey, was also Moderator of the Congress. He passed from one role to the other as it suited him, and the infuriated Governor dissolved the Assembly on April 8 after four days. The Congress re-elected its three delegates to the Continental Congress, approved the nonimportation agreement and authorized Harvey to call another congress when necessary. Martin despondently reported to the Earl of Dartmouth, Secretary of State for the Colonies, that the authority of the royal government was "as absolutely prostrate as impotent and nothing but the shadow of it" left.

News of the battles of Lexington and Concord, fought on April 19, reached North Carolina on May 3. The Committees of Safety at once began to make military preparations. On May 20 the citizens of Mecklenburg County met in Charlotte and issued some "Resolves" which, according to Martin, surpassed "all the horrid and treasonable publications that the inflammatory spirits of this Continent have yet produced." On the twenty-fourth of May, anticipating an attack on his palace in New Bern, Martin sent his pregnant wife and their children off to her father's house, Rockhall, on Long Island, and himself fled to Fort Johnston at the mouth of the Cape Fear River.

In June, the month of the Battle of Bunker Hill and of the appointment of Colonel George Washington to the command of the new continental army by the Congress in Philadelphia, Allan MacDonald called a meeting of the "leading Highlanders."[3] That would include, certainly, Alexander MacLeod, his son-in-law, who was still a lieutenant on half pay; Alexander MacDonald of Cuidreach; Hugh MacDonald of Armadale; Alexander Morrison of Cross Hill, who had come to Cumberland County from Skye in 1772, bringing with him 300 of his neighbors; Murdoch MacLeod, the surgeon of Cross Creek and Anson County; and others: Stewarts, MacRaes, MacArthurs, Camerons, Campbells, MacNeils. Where they met is not recorded, but at that meeting they reached a decision that changed the course of their lives.

It is always puzzling — and even shocking — to Americans that people who had suffered under the Hanoverians, who had endured the atrocities after Culloden, should not, once they were free in a new country, eagerly seize the opportunity to fight for that freedom against their old oppressors. Many, of course, did, but for the most part the Highlanders in North Carolina — and indeed in other parts of America — were Loyalists.

Their reasons were varied and, when examined, understandable. Some of the men, like Alexander MacLeod, were officers on half pay and believed that they owed their loyalty to the British army — and to their half pay. Those who remembered Culloden remembered also the fearful penalties that attended an unsuccessful rebellion against the Hanoverians. Those who came from Argyll had always supported the government. The merchants among them were afraid of losing trade. The North Carolina merchants carried on a prosperous trade directly with England, whereas the New England merchants got their raw materials from the West Indies and had been ruined by the Navigation Acts. Many of the Scots, like Allan himself, had come to North Carolina too recently to have developed firm ties to the land. All of them looked on monarchy as the form of government ordained by heaven and considered republicanism horrid and unnatural. And finally they had, even those who were not new arrivals, that lasting and romantic feeling for Scotland characteristic of Scotsmen everywhere. As Alexander Schaw, Janet's brother and the owner of a large plantation on the Cape

Fear River, wrote to Lord Dartmouth, Secretary of State for the Colonies, "There is now a numerous body of the sons and grandsons of the first Scotch highland settlers, besides the later emigrants, who retain that enthusiastic love for the country from which they are descended, which indeed scarce a highlander ever loses, that they will support its dignity at every risk."[4] Of the humbler Scotsmen, "the common Highlanders," many spoke only Gaelic and obeyed without question the call of their leaders, as they had done from time immemorial.

Duane Meyer in his *The Highland Scots of North Carolina* has pointed out further that "the British in the 18th century were remarkably successful in pacifying former enemies" and he cites as examples the French Canadians and the Scottish Highlanders, both of which groups had recently suffered defeat and yet declined to fight against Britain. The roads and schools that brought the Highlands out of their old isolation, the opportunity to serve in Highland regiments in the Seven Years' War, the increased prosperity had wrought a change in Highland attitudes toward England.[5]

Allan MacDonald's decision had been made swiftly. Flora wrote in 1789 to Sir John MacPherson that Allan, "being a leading man among the Highlanders," was under pressure to join the Rebels and that realizing that he would be obliged to align himself with one side or the other had naturally chosen loyalty to the King. His stand, because of his prestige and Flora's, influenced many of the other Highlanders to join him.

For one or another or a combination of these reasons, the leading Highlanders of North Carolina agreed that they would raise companies to defend the King's interests by force, and that though it would not be prudent to declare their intentions openly at that point they would send word secretly to the Governor to inform him of their purpose and to ask for arms and commissions. Everybody there no doubt intended to be an officer. They delegated Allan — or he offered — to go to Fort Johnston to see the Governor and inform him of their meeting and the readiness of the Highlanders to rise.

So Flora, still in the process of getting settled in the unfamiliar wooden house among the melancholy pines, saw, with what sinking of the heart we can imagine, her husband set out for the distant coast — "in disguise," she said. Someone besides his servant accompanied him, but it was not his son-in-law, for Alexander MacLeod wrote a letter to the Governor which he entrusted to Allan to deliver.

Allan was gone two weeks, on a trip which cost him, he noted carefully, twenty-eight pounds. He spent several days with the Governor at Fort Johnston, the little sand and oyster-shell fort which he had first seen less than a year before when the boat entered the Cape Fear River. It would be hot and steamy in late June and no doubt the mosquitoes were bad. The Governor, harried and worried, keeping up what show of authority he could in his "most despicable and mortifying" situation, was cheered and impressed by Allan's appearance and by the assurances of support from the Highlanders. He wrote to Lord Dartmouth on June 30, proposing to raise a regiment of emigrant troops in North Carolina, asking for 10,000 stand of arms and for his old commission back again. He himself would be colonel of this regiment, and he recommended that Allan be made major and Alexander MacLeod first captain. These two, he declared, "besides being men of great worth and good character, have most extensive influence among the Highlanders here, great part of which are of their own name and familys."[6]

Four days later he wrote a somewhat fulsome letter for Allan to take to Alexander MacLeod.

Sir
　　I had the pleasure of receiving the favour of your letter yesterday by Mr. MacDonald of Kingsborough with whose acquaintance I am so pleased, that I part with him more reluctantly than

I can tell you, & I beg you to be assured that nothing but the opportunity of making a personal acquaintance with that worthy Gentleman, could afford me higher satisfaction than I received from your favour by his hands.

The letter goes on to praise the Highland gentlemen for their good dispositions and to promise to represent their merits faithfully to the King. He continues:

I perfectly agree in your sentiments of the propriety of the good and faithful Highlanders forbearing any open declarations, until there is a necessity to call them into action, and they are amply provided to take the field with dignity and effect. The necessaries for which, I have not omitted to apply for.

He ends by assuring Alexander that the part he had taken did him the highest honor.

I have concerted a Plan with Mr. MacDonald (for which I beg to refer you to him) of making use of your influence here, as well for your own advantage as that of our Royal Masters; and which I shall be happy to find meet with your approbation.

Do me the honour to commend me to your Lady & family in particular, & in general to all the good and faithful Highland People; in whome I have the firmest confidence & for whome I have ever felt peculiar regard & attachment.

I have the honor to be with great respect & esteem
Sir
Your most obedient
& most humble servant
Jo. Martin[7]

Allan's mission quickly became known both to the Loyalists and to the Whigs. On the way to Fort Johnston he evidently stopped in Wilmington, for Janet Schaw wrote in her journal letter:

152

We, the Ladies, adjourned to the house of a Lady, who lived in this street and whose husband was indeed at home, but secretly shut up with some ambassadors from the back settlements on their way to the Govr to offer their service, provided he could let them have arms and ammunition, but above all such commissions as might empower them to raise men by proper authority. This I was presently told tho' in the midst of enemies, but the Loyal party are all as one family.

Allan himself later said that his mission was attended with danger, for two parties were sent out from Wilmington to intercept him. On July third the Wilmington Committee of Safety ordered its chairman to write him a letter, desiring to "know from himself respecting the reports that circulate of his having an intention to raise troops to support the arbitrary measures of the ministry against the Americans in this colony and whether he had not made an offer of his services to Governor Martin for that purpose."[8]

In Wilmington the patriots were drilling in the broiling sunshine. "I must really laugh while I recollect their figures," wrote Miss Schaw, "in their shirts and trousers, preceded by a very ill-beat drum and a fiddler, who was also in his shirt with a long sword and a cue at his hair, who played with all his might. They made indeed a most unmartial appearance. But the worst figure there can shoot from behind a bush and kill even a General Wolfe."

The Whigs too were calling meetings in Anson County, to put the cause of the colonies before the people. Colonel Samuel Spencer attended a meeting on Hedgecock Creek to urge the people to sign the Association of the Congress, that is, the nonimportation agreement, which served as a sort of test oath for patriots. The Scots present objected that many of them had taken an oath of allegiance to the King on their arrival in North Carolina, at the bidding of the Governor and in return for his favors. To this Spencer replied that the

153

oath of allegiance was not binding on them since King George III had himself broken his coronation oath.

As the meetings continued, feeling mounted. Samuel Williams, who went to Governor Martin with a petition and brought back a letter to Allan, had his house broken into by thirty armed men who were infuriated by his report of the "action at Boston [i.e., Bunker Hill] which they said was a most infamous lye and that he was the author."[9]

On the seventh of July Martin sent Alexander Schaw to London with his letter of June 30 and another of July 6 to Lord Dartmouth. Communications even in the most urgent matters were slow and cumbrous. Schaw would have to go first to Boston and there get another boat for England; he would not reach London till October. Copies of Martin's despatches, however, reached Dartmouth in September by other channels and evoked a wry and dampening reply. Martin was not to have his commission back; arms would be sent at General Gage's discretion; it was extremely unlikely, Dartmouth thought, that Martin could induce a large party of North Carolinians to take up arms for the government. It was not until Schaw made his personal appeal in late October that the British Ministry began to take seriously the plan for invading North Carolina and making contact with the loyal Highlanders.

Meanwhile, in the middle of July, Martin left Fort Johnston in the nick of time, before the Wilmington Committee of Safety attacked and burned it, and took refuge on the *Cruizer*, that shabby little sloop of war that had been lying in the river for so long. For the next eleven months he was to be virtually a prisoner, first on the *Cruizer* and then on the *Scorpion*, sending dispatches, receiving letters, entertaining visitors, giving orders — and with difficulty getting enough to eat. He was not alone in his plight; the royal governors of Virginia and South Carolina also spent time on ships-of-war in their respective harbors.

In the back country the slow hot summer wore on. The grain was harvested and their neighbors brought it to the MacDonalds' mill to be ground. The cattle drowsed in the shade of the trees and the July flies sent up their hot rasping drone till midnight. Anne MacLeod, having been delivered of one daughter, was pregnant again. Cuidreach's son Donald, who had reached North Carolina the previous Christmas, was given a plantation on Mountain Creek in Anson County by his grandfather. The family gathered in Hugh's house to witness the signing of the deed.

Young Donald seems to have been well liked by them all. Allan testified some years later that he had known him from his infancy and that his conduct was always "modest and virtuous." His cousin James, Allan's son, found his character "as fair and indisputable as any Gentleman" he was ever acquainted with. The plantation consisted of fifty acres, cleared and fenced, which bore wheat and Indian corn. It already had a dwelling house and outhouses, and Donald proceeded to build a gristmill on the creek. The boy was young, and a man named Daniel Betton managed the plantation for him at first.[10]

In the height of the summer two Highland officers sent by General Gage arrived at Glendale. They had come by ship to Edenton, the northernmost of the three North Carolina seaports; their story that they were on their way to visit their countrymen on the Cape Fear was at first accepted, but on second thoughts the Edenton Committee of Safety, suspecting that "their errand was of a baser nature," wrote to the Committees of Safety of New Bern and Wilmington to "keep a good look out for them." Bypassing Wilmington, they went directly to Cumberland County, where they made their headquarters with Alexander and Anne MacLeod.

They were already known to the people from the islands. Major Donald MacDonald was a cousin of Allan's who had grown up on the tack of Knock, on the east coast of Skye between Portree and Armadale. He had fought at Culloden — and at Bunker Hill. Captain Donald MacLeod, his companion, was of the St. Kilda MacLeods.

They had come to recruit three companies of Highlanders for the Royal Highland Emigrant Regiment which was then being formed in Boston. Allan's Staten Island cousin, Alexander MacDonald, having, as he testified later to the Loyalist Commission, "fled to Boston in the Nick of time when a parcel of low lived rebellious rascals were about to take possession of him and his house," was a captain in the second battalion of this regiment. Major MacDonald offered both Allan MacDonald and Alexander MacLeod captaincies. This put them in something of a quandary, for the Governor had already promised them higher rank in his own regiment, which he had not yet got official permission to raise. They accepted Major MacDonald's proposal on condition that Martin's plan did not go through.

Martin on August 8 issued a proclamation six feet long denouncing the committees of safety, the Mecklenburg Resolves and certain patriots whom he named, and calling on people to be loyal; this, either because of its inflammatory nature or because the Wilmington Committee of Safety had it burned by the hangman, became known as the "Fiery Proclamation." The Whigs firmly believed that he intended to arm the Negroes and free them on condition that they fight for the King, and fright and fury spread through the province. Late in August the Third Provincial Congress met at Hillsboro and decided to raise two regiments for the Continental Army and six battalions of minutemen.

The Congress also appointed a committee of eleven to "confer with the Gentlemen who have lately arrived from the Highlands in Scotland to settle in the Province and to explain to them the Nature of our Unhappy Controversy with Great Britain and to advise and urge to unite with the other Inhabitants of America in defense of those rights which they derive from God and the Constitution." Not only was the committee unsuccessful in shaking Allan and Alexander and the rest, but it lost one of its own members to them, Alexander MacKay, who later became a captain in the Highland battalion.

In the fall Major MacDonald ordered Alexander MacLeod to go to Boston with despatches and reports for General Gage. On the way he stopped at the *Cruizer* to tell the Governor that he and his father-in-law had already raised two companies of Highlanders, and the Governor refused to allow him to leave the province, asserting that his services there were "not to be dispensed with."[11]

Throughout the fall, MacLeod was in close touch with the Governor. If he did not go himself to the *Cruizer*, he sent others with reports of the activities of the Whigs. In October, according to his later report to the Loyalist Commission, he paid "Dr. MacDonald of Cross Creek" (he must have meant Dr. MacLeod, who was the only physician in Cross Creek) fifteen pounds fifteen shillings to take a message, and in November he sent Cuidreach's younger brother Kenneth, now a lieutenant.

When more than three hundred new arrivals came from the Highlands in two successive ships, the Governor gave them — after administering the oath of allegiance — grants of crown land, and Alexander MacLeod further assisted the poorest of them with money "to prevent indigence or ignorance from engaging them to the Rebel party."

Meanwhile, in London, Alexander Schaw had delivered his letters to Lord Dartmouth and made his own persuasive report on the situation in North Carolina. The result was a large and ambitious scheme for the subjugation of the province and, through it, of the rest of the south.

"The King," wrote Dartmouth on October 27, "has thought fit to order that a Body of His Majesty's Forces, consisting of seven Regiments, should prepare to embark at

Cork about the first of December in order to proceed with two companies of Artillery and a proper number of Battalion Guns, Howitzers, etc., to Cape Fear River."[12]

In addition two companies were to be sent from Boston by General Howe, who had succeeded Gage. The fleet from Cork under Sir Peter Parker with seven regiments commanded by Lord Cornwallis, the two companies from Boston and the battalion of Highlanders from the back country were all to converge on Brunswick at the mouth of the Cape Fear and from there to fan out and take possession of both North and South Carolina. The British armies in New England and New York and those in the south would then be in a position to crush the American resistance in the center.

The Loyalists of North Carolina were to play an important part. On November 7 Dartmouth wrote again, directing Martin to lose no time in sending emissaries to the principal persons of trust to tell them to raise as many men as possible. They were to have arms and the same pay as regular troops and they should come down to the coast as soon as they heard of the arrival of British troops there and bring with them a supply of horses and wagons for the use of the army.

Martin, of course, did not receive these orders for several weeks, but the preparations for the Highland rising went steadily on. Alexander MacLeod was busy going back and forth between Anson, Cumberland and Guilford counties at a cost, as he testified later, of fifty-five pounds altogether.

They were hoping to get the Regulators in Orange County to join with the Highlanders. The Regulators were a group of farmers who, ten years earlier, had rebelled against illegal taxes and corrupt tax collectors and against the domination of the rich planters of the eastern districts of the county. Governor Tryon had led two companies of militia against them and had routed them in the Battle of the Alamance, after which victory he departed to be governor of

New York. Martin, succeeding him, had pursued a policy of conciliation toward the Regulators, which he expected to bring them to the side of the King now, reinforced of course by their resentment against the eastern planters who were so active on the American side. But it is not easy to see why he ever thought, as he reported to Dartmouth, that he could raise 3,000 Regulators to fight for the King.

On January 10, 1776, Martin, believing that Cornwallis and his men were on their way from Cork, issued his final Proclamation, calling out the loyal to the King's standard.

Whereas a most daring horrid and unnatural Rebellion has been incited in this Province . . . I found it necessary to Erect his Majesty's Royal Standard and to Collect and Unite the force of His Majesty's faithful People. . . . I do hereby exert and re-quire and Command in the King's name all his Majesty's faithful Subjects on their Duty and Allegiance forthwith to repair to the Royal Standard . . . at the same time pronouncing all such as do not Join the Royal Call as Rebels and Traitors . . . their lives and properties to be forfeited. . . . God Save the King.

To those who remembered Culloden these were powerful words.

14

The Battle of Moore's Creek Bridge

BESIDES the Proclamation, Martin sent, by his agent Alexander MacLean, a despatch to Major Donald MacDonald, now promoted by Martin to brigadier general, commissions for twenty-six Loyalist officers and orders to "concert a place of general rendez-vous thence to march in a body to Brunswick by such route as you shall judge proper, so ordering your movements that you may reach that town on the 15th of February next ensuing."[1] MacLean, who was a British officer on half pay and a merchant of recent arrival in Wilmington, called a meeting of Loyalists in Cross Creek on February 5. All of the Highland leaders showed up and some of the native Loyalists. The Scots were in favor of waiting until the first of March before setting out for Brunswick, unless the British fleet actually arrived earlier, but the Regulators and other Tory leaders wanted immediate action.[2]

Allan MacDonald and Alexander MacLeod had already raised a company apiece; now they had to get together a whole battalion. Alexander MacLeod testified later that he raised a battalion of Highland emigrants in four days. MacLeod, who was better-to-do than his wife's relatives, supplied both Allan and Alexander MacDonald of Cuidreach with money for their expenses in raising men: thirteen pounds ten shillings to Allan, three pounds twelve to Cuidreach. He himself journeyed back and forth between Anson, Cumberland and Guilford counties "on government business with various gentlemen" at a cost of fifty-five pounds.

160

The Battle of Moore's Creek Bridge

They held meetings at different houses throughout Cumberland and Anson counties. The story goes that many of them were "balls" at which Flora MacDonald spoke to the people and fired their enthusiasm. There is no doubt that the respect in which they held her and her husband had a great deal to do with rallying the Highlanders to the King's standard; afterwards some of them held Allan MacDonald responsible for their misery. Martin in a letter to Dartmouth in November had spoken of the influence of Allan Mac-Donald and Alexander MacLeod among the Highlanders and of the jealousy of their superior consequence felt by some of those who had been longer in the country, notably one Farquhard Campbell.[3] Campbell, who had come to North Carolina in 1740 at the age of nineteen, was a member of the Wilmington Committee of Safety and a delegate to all three of the provincial congresses; he found it very difficult to decide where his loyalties lay, served both sides alternately and simultaneously, was imprisoned as a Tory but in the end managed to come down safely on the winning side.

The most important meeting was the one that General MacDonald summoned at Cross Hill on February 10. Cross Hill was the home of Alexander Morrison, about two miles from Glendale in Cumberland County. Morrison was descended through his mother from the nineteenth chief of MacLeod; he had held the tack of Skinidin in Duirinish, Skye, not far from Dunvegan; but in 1771 when his rent had been raised beyond endurance he had gathered together 300 followers and brought them in a body to North Carolina.

Besides the 500 Highlanders who assembled at Cross Hill there were a number of Loyalist leaders who were "country-born," in Allan's phrase, such as Thomas Rutherford, James Cotton and others, who, after being prominent in the provincial congresses and even in the minutemen, decided at the last to stand by the King. Captain Donald MacLeod (now Colonel) appeared at Cross Hill without the

Regulators whom he had been sent to bring in; he had gathered a large group together, he reported, but on the way to Cross Hill they met with a party of Whigs and fled.

Though the number who assembled there was disappointingly small, they decided to hold together and to march on to Cross Creek. Here they were joined by more Highlanders — MacKenzies, MacRaes, MacLeans, MacLauchlans and others — and in the end about 130 Regulators. They had now a grand total of 1,500, of whom only 520 had arms.

The great problem for the Highlanders was the question of arms. Though, as Schaw told Dartmouth, the low-country people all had firearms, the Highlanders, having been disarmed in Scotland, had brought few with them; the Regulators had surrendered theirs to Governor Tryon. Allan and his sons had brought with them their "family arms," evidently fine ones, which, with the arms for their three servants, they valued at over forty-two pounds, but guns and ammunition for the rank and file must be begged or bought. Without the merchants in Cross Creek, who were Highlanders or Highland sympathizers, it could not have been done, but from them supplies of arms, food and clothing were bought and distributed. Alan himself paid for forty-seven pounds' worth of arms, as well as eighteen pounds' worth of shirts, blankets and shoes for "the common Highlanders" and a cask of rum, at seven pounds ten, for the use of the Highlanders on the expedition. Alexander MacLeod provided ninety-one pounds' worth of guns, swords and pistols. In addition, raiding parties were sent out from Cross Creek and they came back with 130 stand of arms seized from the Whigs of the countryside.

The army had a surgeon, Dr. Murdoch MacLeod, and a young chaplain, John Bethune, from Skye.

According to one tradition, when the Highland troops were drawn up to parade at Cross Creek, Flora MacDonald, mounted on a white horse, rode up and down in front of them and addressed them in ringing tones. Another tradition, however, says, "she bade adieu to her husband and relations in arms near her residence in the lower part of Anson County and was not seen in the camp at Cross Creek."[4] This appears to be much more likely, more in harmony with her modest, quiet, steadfast personality.

Some time before February 12, then, she probably stood in the doorway of her home in Anson County and watched her men go off, Allan and their two sons and three manservants. The three MacDonalds rode; they had two "batt-horses" to carry the baggage. The three servants, like the Highlanders who accompanied Boswell and Johnson, ran alongside.

Meanwhile the Whigs, well aware of what was going on, were preparing countermeasures. On February tenth the Committee of Safety of New Bern ordered Colonel Richard Caswell to organize his minutemen. The Wilmington Committee of Safety sent Colonel James Moore with two units of militia and Colonel Alexander Lillington with 150 minutemen up the western side of the Cape Fear to intercept the Highlanders if they should attempt to reach the coast. By February 15, Moore with 1,100 men had camped on Rockfish Creek, eight miles south of Cross Creek, and fortified the bridge.

On February 18, the Highland army of 1,500, in kilts and plaids, with the pipes skirling and the drums rattling, marched out of Cross Creek and camped for the night within four miles of Moore's position. They wanted to reach Brunswick without fighting, if possible, for the men were untrained and only half armed, and there to meet the seven regiments from Cork and the two companies of light infantry from Boston. That Clinton had not left Boston until January 20 and would not reach North Carolina until March

163

and that Cornwallis and his troops were still in Cork, they were happily ignorant.

The next day, after parade and inspection, General Mac-Donald despatched a messenger to Colonel Moore with a flag of truce and copies of Martin's Proclamation and his own Manifesto, urging him to lay down his arms and repair to the King's standard forthwith. Colonel Moore replied by sending General MacDonald the test oath of the Whigs, advising him and all his men to subscribe to it.

After this exchange, MacDonald called his officers together and informed them of the possibility of a battle, whereupon two companies of Colonel Cotton's battalion decided to go home. The next day Farquhard Campbell came to MacDonald and informed him that Caswell with 600 men was marching to join Moore. (Campbell also went to Moore with information about the number and disposition of the Highland army.) MacDonald decided to avoid battle at this stage by going back up the Cape Fear, crossing it near Campbelltown and taking the road down the eastern side of the river; but before he gave the order to march he made a stirring address to the men, calling on all who were not ready to conquer or die to make up their minds now. Twenty more of Colonel Cotton's men declared that their courage was "not war-proof" and left. While Moore was waiting for an attack the Highlanders made their *détente* and got a head start down the other side of the river.

It was February and cold. General MacDonald, who was upwards of seventy, found the long forced march exhausting.

On the twenty-third, the Highlanders again came to a stream to find American forces entrenched on the other side. This time it was the Black River and the troops were Caswell's. They outmaneuvered him by raising a sunken flatboat four miles above the ferry and building a bridge with it, over which they crossed on the morning of the twenty-sixth and marched triumphantly on.

Caswell, when he learned what had happened, sent a messenger to Moore, who ordered him to Moore's Creek Bridge, to meet Lillington there. About twenty miles north of Wilmington the road on the eastern side of the Cape Fear crossed Widow Moore's Creek on a narrow bridge in the middle of a swamp. Caswell and Lillington on the one hand and the Highland army on the other were now all marching toward the bridge.

The Americans got there first. Lillington with 150 men had already camped on the east bank when Caswell with 850 men came up and took command. He had his men build campfires on the west side of the creek and leave them smoldering — a ruse Washington was to use at Trenton — before he joined Lillington on the higher ground of the east bank. There they built earthworks and set up two cannon, known as Mother Covington and her daughter. They then took up the planks in the center of the bridge, greased the sleepers with tallow and poured soft soap on them, and retired behind their fortifications to wait.

The Highlanders stopped six miles from Moore's Creek Bridge for a council of war. Their elderly general was worn out and ill; he could go no farther. They put him to bed in a tent and the remaining leaders conferred. Scouts who had been sent ahead having reported that Caswell was encamped in an exposed position on the west side of the creek, the younger officers, led by Colonel Donald MacLeod, were all for making an attack on him at once, and in spite of the caution of the older men they prevailed.

At one o'clock on the cold, cloudy morning of February 28 the advance began, led by seventy-five picked men with broadswords, Colonel MacLeod at their head. They plunged and floundered through the swamp in silence. When the sky was turning gray, they came on the smoldering fires near the bridge, and thinking that Caswell had abandoned his camp, they took heart and rushed forward, not sure in the dark just where the bridge was. Suddenly MacLeod shouted, "King George and broadswords!" and the pipers and drummers broke into shrill and stirring sound.

MacLeod led the charge on the bridge; others crowded on his heels. After the first few planks the bridge was nothing but two slippery poles and a gaping hole. The Americans behind their earthworks opened fire. Mother Covington and her daughter spoke. Donald MacLeod got across the bridge by digging the point of his sword into the greased sleeper but fell as he struggled up the bank. Fifty others sliding and stumbling in the morning twilight, tumbling headlong into the creek, were shot or drowned. In three minutes of noise, confusion and anguish, the Highlanders fought — and lost — the Battle of Moore's Creek Bridge. Those Scots who had not got onto the bridge turned and ran; those who could get hold of horses, it was said, went off helter-skelter, three on a horse.

Allan MacDonald said afterwards that he had had the honor to be in command that day, and he described the engagement as a "check."[5] With General MacDonald ill in a tent six miles away and Colonel MacLeod lying dead on the creek bank, Allan succeeded in command. When the officers managed to stop the flight of the soldiers and hold a council, it must have been Allan's voice that gave the orders to march up the river again to Smith's Ferry, beyond Cross Creek, and from there let each man get home as best he could. He paid for food for them on the march back.

The Americans did not pursue them immediately, being much too busy gathering up the baggage and plundering the wagons that had been left behind. When Moore joined them a few hours later he ordered pursuit. One detachment took General MacDonald prisoner; the rest caught up with the fleeing Highlanders near Black Mingo Creek, only a few miles away. They held the officers but set free the common soldiers, after administering the oath of allegiance to them. Allan was taken prisoner, with both his sons; so were Alexander of Cuidreach and his brothers, James and Kenneth, the aide-de-camp to General MacDonald. Alexander Mac-Leod escaped into the swamps and so, after a few days, did Allan's younger son James.

In the three-minute battle the 1,500 Highlanders lost 50 killed or wounded, 850 prisoners; the 1,100 Whigs had one man killed, one wounded. The Whigs claimed to have captured 350 guns and shot bags, 1,500 excellent rifles, 150 swords and dirks, 13 wagons with horses, two medicine chests and 15,000 pounds sterling. 'In view of the repeated statements that only half of the Highlanders were armed, one wonders where those 1,500 rifles came from. Doubt about the rifles also casts doubt on the large sum of sterling claimed, since Allan and Alexander had had to contribute to the purchase of necessities. There is no question about the medicine chests, which belonged to Dr. Murdoch MacLeod, who had an apothecary shop in Cross Creek.

The Battle of Moore's Creek Bridge was the first battle in the Revolution in which the American side had a decisive victory. The Battle of Lexington and Concord was more a psychological than a military success, and Bunker Hill was a noble defeat. Moore's Creek was the turning point in North Carolina. If the Highlanders had won, it is estimated that some 10,000 who were doubtful would have joined them, and Clinton and Cornwallis, arriving tardily in March and May respectively, would have taken North Carolina for the King. The confidence which their success gave to the Americans led the North Carolina Provincial Congress to be, in April, 1776, the first official body in America to vote explicitly for independence.[7]

15

Aftermath

FLORA MacDonald wrote her own account of the Battle of Moore's Creek Bridge to Sir John MacPherson. What she said about the battle was written from hearsay and the numbers were exaggerated — she pictured the Highland army marching 200 miles and meeting 3,000 Congress troops — but her account of her own misfortunes and struggles in the two years following the battle is straight from experience and is the only direct report of it that remains.

"Mr. MacDonald and about 30 other Gentlemen were draged from goal to goal for 700 miles," she wrote bitterly,

till lodged in Philadelphia Goal, remaining in their hands for 18 months before exchanged. Mrs. Flora McDonald being all this time in misery and sickness at home, being informed that her husband and friends were all killed or taken, contracted a severe fever, and was dayly oppressed with stragling partys of plunderers from their Army, and night robbers who more than once threatened her life, wanting a confession where her husbands money was. Her servants deserted her, and such as stayed grew so very insolent that they were of no service to her.[1]

From other sources it is clear that after the Battle of Moore's Creek Bridge, the North Carolina countryside was filled with unrest; there were rumors of Tory uprisings; bands of Whigs — and also of Tories — descended on the farms, frightening the women and children, looting and plundering in the name of their committees or of their superior officers. The Committees of Safety themselves were concerned in the first year or two of the war to protect the weak and helpless. When, on May 1, 1776, the North Carolina Provincial Congress appointed commissioners in six counties, including Anson and Cumberland, to take inventories of the estates of the prisoners of Moore's Creek Bridge, it instructed them "at the same time to pay particular attention to the unhappy women and children to see that they do not want the common necessaries of life."[2]

When these Commissioners came to Flora's farm to take an inventory, she evidently stood up to them with considerable courage. She says nothing of them in her report to Sir John MacPherson, but she or someone else managed to let Allan know about it, for his cousin Captain MacDonald, writing to him from Nova Scotia more than a year later, commented admiringly, "I am happy to hear of Mrs. MacDonald's Welfare & her Spirited behavior when brot before the Committee of Rascals in North Carolina. I don't doubt but She & the Other Gentlewomen there will be sorely oppressed by the Savage Cruelty of those Wretches who at present has the Upper hand of them."[3]

The gentlemen of the Congress sought to be humane and enlightened, in the eighteenth-century concept of warfare, but at the local level, as always, there were bands of violent and greedy men who were far less concerned with the cause than with plunder. There are numerous stories of harried people taking to the woods and swamps when the marauding bands arrived. The families of Dr. Murdoch MacLeod and of Kenneth Black both suffered in this way and, closer to home, Flora's own daughter and her half sister Annabella.

It was natural enough, but an added grief, that many of the women who lived in fear and misery in the back country blamed Allan MacDonald for having got them into this mess.

"When she got the better of her fever," Flora wrote,

she went to visit & comfort the other poor Gentlewomen whose Husbands were prisoners with Mr. MacDonald, as they blamed him as being the author of their misery, in riseing the highlanders and in one of these charitable visits, fell from her horse and brock her right arm, which confined her for months; the only phisytian in the collony being prisoner with her husband in Philadelphia goals having no comforter but a young boy her Son, the oldes Alex^r being prisoner with his father.

James was eighteen or nineteen at this time, hardly a "young boy" in an age when boys of fifteen had their commissions and fought, but he was the youngest of her children in America and perhaps still seemed to her the baby of the family.

"She remained in this deplorable condition for two years, among Robers and faithless servants."

In 1777 the North Carolina Congress required everyone in the state to take the oath of allegiance, and those who refused had their estates confiscated. At this time Flora lost the plantation in Anson and moved into Cumberland, staying, so a firm tradition declares, on one of Kenneth Black's farms, either near Anne MacLeod at Glendale or near Annabella at Mt. Pleasant.

Anne, too, had suffered. Her husband, after the battle, had hidden for six weeks in the woods and swamps before he had managed to make his way to Governor Martin on the *Scorpion*. When Sir Henry Clinton came with his 200 men from Boston, Alexander joined him and went with him to New York. Rewards were offered for him by the Americans and his property was plundered, fifteen hundred pounds' worth carried off or destroyed. Anne, who was pregnant and nearing her time, fled "to a near relative's house, twenty-four miles away." This may have been Annabella, or Flora after she had left Anson County. Anne's children, two boys and a girl, the eldest six at the most, were hidden in the woods by their nurses, who, when found and questioned, declared the children to be their own. A manservant was "almost strangled to death in order to discover his master's effects."[4] MacLeod's servants were faithful, if Flora's were not. The expected baby, a second girl, was safely born in spite of the flight and fear, and at length help came.

"Her husband and son-in-law, Major Alex^r MacLeod," wrote Flora, "obtained a flag of truce from Sir Henry Clinton and Admiral How, which brought me, my Daughter and her children from Wilmington in N. Carolina to New York."

On February 21, 1778, Alexander himself arrived on the sloop *Sukey and Peggy* in the lower Cape Fear, and before anyone could stop him he had gone ashore at Brunswick and tried to buy some fresh meat. Colonel Ward of the North Carolina militia at once put a guard on the sloop to prevent Alexander from communicating with any of his friends, and he and General John Ashe both sent anxious reports to Governor Richard Caswell (the former Colonel Caswell, hero of Moore's Creek Bridge). Three local patriots, also much exercised, wrote to Caswell, "We must beg to acquaint you that Major MacLeod, who brings the Flag, was one of the principal acting officers in the Insurrection in this State by the Highlanders and was himself in the engagement at Widow Moore's Creek."[5]

The Governor and his council at New Bern were inclined to take a calmer view of this invasion. Major MacLeod's despatches to Mrs. MacLeod and Mrs. MacDonald must be read, they directed, by Colonel Ward or General Ashe, whose vigilance would "prevent any bad effects from the landing at Brunswick." The flag of truce was considered a proper one, and Major MacLeod was to be given leave to "carry out with his wife and son and Mrs. MacDonald and her four children with their indentured female servants." The Governor confused the families; the son was Flora's, the four children, Anne's. MacLeod was directed by the Governor to send word to his wife and mother-in-law "of his arrival and of their having leave to depart the State"; a guard was to be continued on the *Sukey and Peggy* as long as she lay in the Cape Fear, and nobody on board the sloop was to go on shore or have any communication with the people on shore; and, finally, Major MacLeod was to be told "that the more expeditious he is in getting away, the greater satisfaction he will give the State."[6]

Where he found the messengers to go to the back country and escort his family to Brunswick is not recorded, but it cost him one hundred thirty pounds to remove his family to New York and only fifty pounds to send them to England six months later.

Though James was included in the passport, he does not seem to have gone to New York with Flora. He and his cousin Donald fought together, he declared in 1784, in the same corps in different actions in the Carolinas. Donald, the son of Cuidreach and Annabella, who did not take part in the Moore's Creek Bridge campaign, testified that he hid in the swamps after "several tempting offers were made to him to take a commission in the American army which he refused with silent indignation." In 1780, when the British had invaded South Carolina, Donald got an ensign's commission in Tarleton's famous green-coated British Legion, and pre-satisfaction he will give the States."[6]

After a miserable voyage up the coast from Brunswick to New York, "in the dead of winter, being in danger of our lives for the most of the voyage by a constant Storm," Flora, her daughter and son-in-law and their four children safely reached New York, where she and Allan were after more than two years reunited.

ᔍ 16 ᔍ

Allan's Adventures

ALLAN MacDonald, who had been waiting eagerly to welcome his wife and children, had himself had two years of considerable stress.

He was captured by Caswell's men a day or two after the battle; his horse, his arms and his baggage were taken from him and he was marched on foot along the crude road through the woods to Halifax, where he was thrown into "the common jail" with a number of others.

Halifax, North Carolina, was a prosperous trading center on the Dan River fifteen miles from the Virginia border. It had a courthouse, an inn, an assembly hall, a jail and some fifty stores and dwellinghouses. The jail, which is still standing, was a small two-story brick box; the thirty or more Highland officers who were crowded into it in early March, without blankets, bedding or any sort of fire, must have been miserably uncomfortable as well as humiliated.

Soon after Allan reached Halifax, along with his son Alexander, his brother-in-law Cuidreach, Cuidreach's two brothers, James and Kenneth, also Dr. MacLeod and Chaplain Bethune, he was joined by General Donald MacDonald. It had taken Caswell's men little time to find the General in his sickbed and make him a prisoner. A party of horsemen took him on February 28 to Caswell's camp, where he formally surrendered his sword to General Moore, "who was pleased to deliver [it] back in a genteel manner before all his officers then present according to the rules and customs of war practised in all nations."[1] At this point the gentility ran out. After rummaging through his papers they bundled him first to New Bern and thence to Halifax; his horses, saddles and pistols were taken from him and he was committed on his arrival, as he complained, "in a sickly state of health and immediately ushered into a common gaol without bed or bedding, fire or candles in a cold long night, by Colonel Long, who did not appear to me to behave like a gentleman."[2] Both he and Allan, however, were allowed to keep their servants, a concession which must have eased the situation considerably.

General MacDonald was released on parole after being in the jail for a month. By this time the fourth North Carolina Provincial Congress was meeting in Halifax, and it took time from its other business "on consideration of the candor of Allan MacDonald and his being in a low state of health" to admit him to parole on the same terms as General MacDonald. A few days later Allan's son Alexander was also paroled. The terms of the parole included the usual provisions, staying within the town limits, holding no conversations with the enemy, reporting each day to the officer of the guard.

The Congress, exhilarated by the success of Moore's Creek Bridge, issued in this month of April, 1776, what became known as the Halifax Resolutions, in which they recommended complete independence from England three months before the Continental Congress in Philadelphia.

The Halifax Committee of Safety, saddled with the uncomfortable burden of the prisoners of war, looked about for a way to pass it along to other hands. On April 22 the Committee decided to send the prisoners taken "in the late commotion" to Maryland, Virginia and Philadelphia and to let the authorities in those places cope with them. The twenty-six most influential prisoners were to go to Philadelphia. At the top of the list was General Donald MacDonald; next to him, Colonel Allan MacDonald of Kingsburgh, second in command. Kingsburgh's son Alexander, MacDonald of Cuidreach, Kenneth MacDonald, Murdoch MacLeod the surgeon and John Bethune the chaplain, as well as Farquhard Campbell, were also among the twenty-six. The letter to John Hancock, President of the Continental Congress, explaining the action, shows that for all their victory over the Highlanders, the North Carolinians were still apprehensive about invasion. Sir Henry Clinton had by this time come and gone, but Lord Cornwallis was nearing the coast.

We are sorry to be compelled to an act of such severity as this of sending these men at such a distance from their unfortunate families; but the security of our country makes it indispensably necessary for should they have an opportunity of exerting their pernicious influence at a time when we may be invaded by a powerful army, the consequences might, and probably would, prove fatal.[3]

The march of the prisoners began on April 25. The first stop was Petersburg, Virginia. Only a year or two earlier an Englishman making the trip from Halifax to Petersburg had described it as "a most unpleasant journey; bad accommodations, bad roads, bad company and attendance, and in short everything disagreeable in the extreme."[4] And he rode. The prisoners went on foot.

From Petersburg Allan wrote on May 2 a letter of protest to a friend who had sent him some Virginia money. He objected to being confined under guard in a room with General MacDonald when both of them had been on parole in Halifax; he added, "I have also been depressed of the horse I held and hath little chance of getting another. To walk on foot is what I can never do the length of Phila-delphia."[5] (He meant, all the way to Philadelphia.) But walk he did, nevertheless, from Petersburg to Fredericksburg, to Alexandria, to Baltimore, to Philadelphia, and he was later in life to complain that the hardships he suffered during his imprisonment resulted in his losing the use of his legs.

On May 25 the Committee of Safety of Pennsylvania informed the Congress that the prisoners from North Carolina had arrived, that they had ordered them to be closely confined, that they had appointed an officer guard for them, and inquired what subsistence was to be granted them. The Continental Congress, sitting in the State House, the building not yet known as Independence Hall, approved the action of the Committee of Safety and granted the officers an allowance of two dollars a week for board and lodging, which was to be repaid by the prisoners when they should be released. The day when a prisoner became the guest of the state was still in the future; the two-dollar allowance was only a loan, which the officers would repay out of their accumulated pay when they could get it.

They were confined in the New Gaol on Walnut Street at Sixth, directly across the square from the State House. It was so new, in fact, that it still lacked locks, bolts and bars, and Mr. William Rush was directed to have a sufficient number made immediately.

General MacDonald lost no time in protesting his imprisonment. "General MacDonald wishes to know," he inquired icily on May 29, after recapitulating his experiences after the battle and reminding them that he had been paroled, "what crime he has since been guilty of, deserving his being recommitted to the jail of Philadelphia without his bedding or baggage and his sword and servant detained from him. The other gentlemen prisoners are in great want for their blankets and other necessities."[6]

The Continental Congress, though it later restored his and Allan's servants and provided blankets and other necessaries, had at the moment other business to attend to, such

176

as the matter of flints for the muskets for the troops and the still more pressing resolution of independence, which they debated warmly all through June. The gentlemen-prisoners remained in the new prison, which was built handsomely of stone and stretched from Walnut Street through to Prune, now Locust. Those whose windows looked north could see the brick building with the bell tower across the square and the members of the Congress coming and going.

On July 4 Congress ordered "that application be made to the Committee of Safety of Pennsylvania for a supply of flints for the troops at New York," after which they resolved themselves into a committee of the whole to vote on a Declaration of Independence prepared by Mr. Thomas Jefferson. Immediately after the amended Declaration had been passed, the Congress returned to the flints. After determining to send a man at public expense to Orange County for a sample of flint stone, they appropriated "3 dollars and 54 ninetieths" for the expenses of a messenger who brought despatches from Trenton. And at length they wound up the day by resolving that Dr. Franklin, Mr. J. Adams and Mr. Jefferson be a committee to prepare a device for a seal for the United States of America. This was the first time that the name of the new-created nation was used in an official action.[7]

The Declaration of Independence was read publicly four days later, and the prisoners in the jail may have wondered why they heard the bell ringing so loudly. It was not until August 2 that, the Declaration having been engrossed on parchment, the members of Congress actually signed it,[8] signing their lives into jeopardy and their faith into fact. But by then Allan MacDonald and his son were no longer in Philadelphia. They had been released on parole on July 9, with the understanding that they go to Reading in Berks County and remain there until they could be exchanged.

Reading, a small town fifty-five miles up the Schuylkill

River from Philadelphia, was humming with activity. Throughout the war it was used, to the annoyance of its inhabitants, as a center for prisoners, especially Hessians. Allan and his son were the only two of the North Carolina Highlanders to be sent there; they had an allowance of five dollars a week for board and lodging for themselves and Allan's servant, and that was sometimes late in arriving.[9]

General Donald MacDonald was exchanged in December, 1776, but Allan and Alexander were kept on in Reading all through the winter and spring. In April Allan wrote a petition to John Hancock, President of the Congress, asking again for exchange and pointing out that inflation had made the five-dollar allowance inadequate. "Drink, Lodging and Cloathing and in short everything is so extravagantly high priced that Prisoners must be in a very miserable State, Two dollars, the common allowance per week, being of greater service ten months before now, than Six these days."[10]

He was able none the less to replenish his wardrobe. In May he was ordering from a merchant on Market Street in Philadelphia material for two pairs of breeches "of wheat corded or plain stuff" and material for two summer waistcoats and half a yard of scarlet stuff with the necessary "furniture."[11]

He was still in Reading in July, still hoping for exchange and urging that his good behavior and his son's should be considered in this connection. The trouble was the question of rank. The Americans wanted to exchange him for a Colonel Lute then on parole in Reading; the British preferred to consider him a captain and to yield only a captain for him. The letter that he wrote to the Congress on July 18, 1777, is interesting for its mention of Flora.

Now, sir, permit me to say: when you'll know the dispersed and distress't state of my family you will at least sympathize with me and pity my oppress'd mind. I am here with one of my Sons — seventeen months a Prisoner. My wife in North Carolina 700 miles from me in a very sickly tender state of health, with a younger Son, a Daughter, & four Grand Children. Two Sons in our Service of whom I heard little or nothing, since one of them had been wounded in the Battle of Bunkers hill — and two in Britain, of whom, I heard no account since I left it. Them in Carolina I can be of no service to in my present state, but were I Exchanged I would be of service to the rest if in life.[12]

The son wounded at Bunker Hill may have been Charles, who had left the East India Service and gone into the army. Ranald was with the marines under Lord Rodney.

Allan stated in this petition that he was a lieutenant colonel in the North Carolina militia but a captain in the regular army and that he was sure that Sir William Howe would exchange him in either rank; he asked to be sent to General Howe to negotiate his own exchange and his son's. On August 21 the Congress freed him for this purpose, and by September 15 Governor Martin, now with his wife's family on Long Island, was writing to Lord George Germain that Allan MacDonald had recently arrived in New York.

New York, with Staten Island and Long Island, was occupied by British troops at that time, but Howe was not there. He, with Cornwallis and his regiments, was in Pennsylvania engaged in winning the Battle of the Brandywine. Allan accomplished his exchange nevertheless and got in touch with his cousin Captain MacDonald, who was now in Halifax.

On October 18 the Captain wrote to him, "I am extremely happy to hear that you and yr Son were safe in New York." He continued with the news that Ranald and Charles were both in Halifax and "very happy at the Thoughts of seeing you soon." He urged Allan to come to Halifax before the winter set in and gave him what must have been a welcome report on the amount of accumulated pay on which he could draw.[13]

Allan stayed on in New York, in spite of his cousin's

urging, to raise a company of Highlanders and to arrange for Flora to be brought there. In December Captain MacDonald sent him a letter which was to be delivered by Ranald himself. "He is a fine young fellow and will make an Excellent Officer if he lieves. You tell me," added the Captain severely, "you have contracted a great Deal of Debt. I dare Saie you have lieved Expensive but it is High time now my dear Allan to Study Oeconomy." Then he added, "Pray for God's sake is it possible to Gett Mrs. McDonald & the other poor women from N. Carolina?"[14]

During the winter Charles and Ranald, who were lieutenants, pressured their father to buy higher commissions for them, to their cousin's disapproval. "Charles is a fine young fellow for whom I have the sincerest regard but the income of a General Offr wd be rather small for him if he could get it, he is very Sensible and very Clever when sober but rather unhappy when he is anyways disguised in Liquor but yr presence here might be the means of altering it and putting a stop to it."[15] A month later he was writing even more forcibly, "One thing I am sure of, it is absolutely necessary that you should be as near them [Charles and Ranald] as possible to overaw their Conduct and assist them with good Advice."[16]

Allan, however, was waiting in New York for Flora.

Back to Skye

FROM April to August, 1778, a good part of the family was together in New York: Flora and Allan and Alexander, Anne and Alexander MacLeod and their four children. Allan was busy with his company of eighty-four "gentlemen volunteers," whom he dressed in a smart uniform of scarlet and blue,[1] and deaf to his cousin's increasingly impatient demands that he come to Halifax, Nova Scotia, and join the 84th Regiment, of which Allan was now a captain. From the point of view of the Highland refugees from North Carolina, New York was much nearer their relatives who were still struggling in the sand hills — Flora's son James, her father, who was to die in Anson County in 1780, her sister Annabella and her children — than Nova Scotia was.

New York in the hot and sticky summer of 1778 was in the hands of Sir Henry Clinton, who had come from Philadelphia at the end of June, pursued by Washington and his troops fresh from Valley Forge. All around the city the Americans sat waiting apprehensively for the British to attempt a march up the Hudson to split New England from the middle states or to take ship for an attack on Charles Town or Savannah. When they finally did, in November, embark for Savannah, Alexander of Cuidreach, exchanged after more than two years, went with them.

Flora and Allan stayed in New York as long as they could, but finally, on August 21, Captain MacDonald threatened to stop Allan's credit if he did not come soon.[2] Allan perforce handed his company over to a "young gentleman whom he appointed to the command" and departed for Halifax and the 84th Regiment. Flora was "obliged tho' tender to follow and was very nigh death's door by a violent disorder the Rough Sea and long passage had brought on."[3]

Possibly her son Alexander was with her, but her daughter Anne was not. In the same month, October, Alexander MacLeod was sent with despatches to London, and he took his family with him. Though he had joined Sir Henry Clinton at the Cape Fear in April, 1776, he had found when he reached New York that through some confusion the commission that he had expected was not forthcoming and that he was relegated to being an officer on half pay. In London he spent seven months presenting his claims for the expenses he had incurred in raising the Highlanders in North Carolina and pressing for his commission, which he finally succeeded in getting. By 1780 he was back in America, fighting under Cornwallis in campaigns in the Carolinas.

When Flora reached Halifax after an uncomfortable passage of at least two weeks in the autumn storms, she found that the detachment of the 84th Regiment to which Allan was assigned had moved to Fort Edward at Windsor, forty-five miles away.

"At last landing in Halifax," she wrote, "were allowed to stay there for eight days on account of my tender state, the ninth day sett out for Windsor on the bay of Minos throw woods and snow and arived the fifth day."

The road from Halifax to Windsor, which was actually situated on the river Avon, eight miles fom its mouth at the Basin of Minas, off the Bay of Fundy, lay through the winter woods — snow-laden spruces, pines and dwarf birches at first, then beeches, maples, elms — until, crossing a ridge, it came down on fertile lands where formerly the French had planted farms and orchards and raised enough wheat to send all the way to Boston.

"There," wrote Flora, "we continued all winter and

spring, covered with frost and snow and almost starved with cold to death, it being one of the worst winters ever seen there."

Allan's cousin, who commanded the second battalion of the Regiment, was there with Susie his wife — "my fat frow," as he called her with offhand affection — who was pregnant, and three of their five children. The two eldest boys had been sent to Edinburgh for their education.

Fort Edward was dull as well as cold, and the young officers, who included Alexander and Charles, languished for the comparative gaiety of Halifax, which as well as being a naval base was the capital of the province. Captain Mac-Donald wrote to his superior officer in December:

Our young fellows are so fond of dancing and seeing the ladies at Halifax they are constantly plaguing me for leave to go down there and they'll think it hard when I refuse them. I have given leave to Lieut. Alexander Macdonald to convey his Brother Lieut. Charles as far as Halifax and ordered him immediately upon his Arrival to wait upon you for Approbation to stay a few days.[4]

On the nineteenth of January, 1779, Captain MacDonald's wife Susie gave birth in the cold northern outpost to her sixth child; both mother and child died. The Captain was desolated; his hearty, bluff, somewhat coarse letters come to an end after this blow. Flora must have given help and comfort to the Captain and his little brood.

She survived the winter and the long cold spring; in the neighborhood of Windsor it is still remembered that once she lived there.

Other friends from North Carolina were in Nova Scotia at this time: Cuidreach's brother Kenneth, who had been aide-de-camp to General MacDonald at Moore's Creek Bridge, and the Reverend John Bethune, who was now chaplain to the 84th Regiment. He was to stay on in Canada after the war and to establish the first Presbyterian church in Montreal.

In the summer of 1779 Flora had another fall, dislocating her good wrist and tearing some tendons. Though she was under the care of the regimental surgeon, it was two months before her wrist was usable again. Homesickness now swept over her. Ranald was off at sea with Rodney; James was with the British army somewhere in South Carolina; Anne was in London. Johnny and Fanny she had not seen in five years. Desperately she longed to leave this cold strange flat country and go home to the hills of Skye.

Allan got a berth for her on the *Lord Dummore,* a privateer of 24 guns, and with three young ladies and two gentlemen she set sail for London in October, 1779. There is a persistent legend, which is perpetuated in an inscription in the Episcopal church at Portree, Skye, that on the voyage this ship was attacked by a French privateer and that Flora "encouraged the sailors to make a spirited and successful resistance, thus risking her life for both the Houses of Stuart and Hanover." The truth, as usual, is quieter and more in keeping with her character. "In our passage," she wrote, "spying a sail, made ready for Action and in Hurrying the ladys below, to a place of Safety, my foot skiping a Step in the trap fell and brock the dislockated arm in two it was sett with bandages over slips of wood and keep my bed till we arived in the Thames."[5] But it is clear that it was she who was shepherding the other ladies, taking responsibility for the safety of others.

The broken arm set by unskilled hands with a makeshift split must have caused her considerable pain, but when she reached London a greater anguish was to greet her, the news of her son Alexander's death at sea. "To my great sorrow, on my landing, received the melancholy newes of my son

Alex^r's death, Lieut. of Light Infantry, being lost on his way home haveing got lieve on account of his bad state of health, an old wound constantly breaking out, from the fatigue of the light-infantry Service brought him very lowe."[6] This is all that is known of his wound, which presumably was incurred at the Battle of Moore's Creek.

Writing more than nine years later of the bad news that met her on her arrival in London, she telescoped two events and ascribed to this time a tragedy that actually occurred more than two years later, the loss of Ronald in the *Ville de Paris*. "And a short time thereafter," she wrote,

got the accounts of the *Ville de Paris* being lost, on her way home, where my beloved son Ranald was Captain of mareens haveing served in Lord Rodney's ship, everywhere he was. These melancholy Strocks, by the death of my Children who, had they lived, with God's assistance, might now be my support in my declined old age, brought on a violent fitt of sickness, which confined me to my bed in London, for half a year, and would have brought me to my Grave, if under God's hands, Doctor Donald Munrow had not given his friendly assistance.[7]

Dr. Munro was a son of Professor Alexander Munro of Edinburgh University and related through his mother to Sir Alexander MacDonald of Sleat.

It is not known with whom she stayed during this time of illness. Lady Margaret MacDonald, who must have been about seventy by this time, was living in London in Welbeck Street. A sister of Captain MacDonald's had come up to London with her, and the Captain himself felt close enough to Lady Margaret to write her a voluminous account of the wrongs which he considered that he had suffered in the army, but Flora for some reason seems not to have felt free to go to her. Lady Primrose, who had been so generous to her, had died in 1775. But she had some friend or relative, probably from the islands, who took her in and ministered to her.

Flora stayed in London until May, 1780, and then at last she set out for Skye. She stopped first in Edinburgh, where she saw Mrs. John MacKenzie, the widow of the MacDonalds' devoted old friend, MacKenzie of Delvine. Perhaps too she saw her son Johnny, whom the MacKenzies had educated. He won a cadetship in the Bombay Infantry in 1780, but it is possible that he had not yet departed for India.

From Edinburgh on May 17 Flora wrote a letter to a merchant in Glasgow asking him to transfer her baggage to the Long Island, where she was going to stay with her cousin MacDonald of Boisdale. This was the son of Alexander MacDonald of Boisdale, who had visited and helped Charles Edward Stuart when he was hiding in Glen Corradale and whose arrest had warned the Prince's followers that it was time to get him off the Long Island. The baggage that Flora was concerned about contained the few things that she had been able to salvage from the plantation in Anson County, which Allan in his claim to the Loyalist Commission valued at forty pounds.

"It is recommended to me by my Physicians," Flora wrote, "to make all possible speed to the highlands for the benefite of the goat Whey. I mean to go to Skye by Inverness as being the most expeditious way. I propose to take up my residence in the Long Island."[8]

Goat whey, according to Martin, the traveler whom Dr. Johnson read with so much interest, could be boiled up with violets to make a sovereign remedy for fevers — which suggests that Flora's ailment was one of those recurring fevers which people picked up in the autumn in coastal North Carolina.

She left Edinburgh early in July, 1780, and on the twelfth she wrote from Dunvegan to Mrs. MacKenzie:

Back to Skye

I arrived at Inverness the third day after parting with you in good health and without any accidents, which I always dread. My young Squire continued always very obliging and attentive to me. [She did not name the "young Squire," but it is possible that it was Johnny himself, riding with his mother as far as Inverness.] I stayed at Inverness three days. I had the good luck to meet with a female companion from that to Skye. I was the fourth day with great difficulty at Raasay, for my hands being so pained with the riding. I have arrived here a few days ago with my young daughter.[8]

She was at home again, at last.

✿ 18 ✿

The Closing Years

THE young daughter, of course, was Fanny, now "a stout Highland 'Caileag' quite overgrown of her age,"[1] which was just fourteen. Flora had picked her up in Raasay and brought her to Dunvegan, the centuries-old castle of the MacLeods on the west coast of Skye.

The young chief of MacLeod had in 1776, at the age of twenty-two, given up the struggle with rents and tenants and debts and gone into the army. As a captain in the well-known regiment, Fraser's Highlanders, he went to America and fought there until 1781, when he was transferred to India. In his absence he invited his uncle and his wife to stay at Dunvegan until Alexander MacLeod could establish a home for his family.

Flora and Fanny stayed with Anne for a time before they went on to the Long Island, where they visited Flora's brother at Milton, her cousin at Loch Boisdale, and spent some time at Kirkibost in North Uist with the Mrs. MacDonald who had been at Mugstot on the first of July in 1746 and with whom Flora had ridden away while her gawky maid Betty Burke shocked the churchgoing countryfolk by lifting her skirts too high when she straddled the brook. Flora was again staying at Kirkibost the following year, when letters came to her that filled her with tremulous hope for her son Alexander. She wrote to a cousin, Donald MacDonald of Balranald:

Dr Sir

I cannot bout atempt writing you the unexpected, joyeful news I received this day from Ranald, dated October the 16, from New York about my Dr. Sandy. I shall give it you in his own words, you will be no doubt much surprised to hear that Sandy is still in the land of the living, they were taken up at sea by a vessel from lisbone, and carey'd to the Coast of Brasil, this news put me in such confution that I can scarce hold the pen. I have great reason to be thankfull for all their preservation. He writs me that he got a letter from his father in June from Halifax and that he was then in very good health and that Charles and James was well, he regrets that his Brave Captain lost his Leg, his ship suffered greatly. This is two Letters I receiv'd from him within this ten days, he writs me that General Clinton with 6 thousand men was going to embark to assist Lord Cornwales, who was blocked up by the French fleet, they had 28 sail, the Enemy 34 Sail of the line of Battle-Ships. God send us good account of them. God bless him poor man he never refuses an oppertunity in writing to his Mother I am very glad to hear that the Children are upon the mending hand, the major desires to be kindly re-membered to you and Mrs. McDonald, youl

except of the same from
your affectionate
Cousin F mcD[2]

Kirkibost the 10 of December
1781

After this happy news about Sandy, nothing more was heard from him, and gradually hope dwindled and died.

Four months later, on April 12, 1781, Ranald was in the Battle of the Saints, so called because it took place near a little group of islands in the Caribbean between Guadeloupe and Dominica. After a full day of fighting in the largest naval engagement in eighty years, Rodney defeated de Grasse, capturing his 120-gun flagship, the *Ville de Paris*, and with it the French admiral himself. Ranald survived the battle, but on the way back to England with the captured ship he was lost with all on board when the *Ville de Paris,* which had been damaged in the battle, foundered and sank. The news must have reached Flora early that summer. Both she and Allan seem to have felt an especial tenderness for Ranald. Three years later Allan wrote, "What added to the utter misery of your Memorialist was the loss of his third son, Captain Ranald MacDonald of Marines in the Ville de Paris, having served all the time of the war under lords Rodney and Hood."

In 1782 Flora wrote from Milton, "I am now in my brother's house, on my way to Skye to attend my daughter, who is to ly in in August." Allan was still in Halifax. When the war came to an end in 1783 and the 84th Regiment was disbanded, he received a regimental grant of land in Nova Scotia, 3,000 acres on the Kennetcook River, not far from Windsor. He cleared some of the land and built a "small neat hutt" before he decided that to develop it properly he needed capital.

In 1784 he went to London, to file his claim for the losses he had sustained in North Carolina with the Commission on Loyalist Claims, which had been established to review the claims of those who had lost money and land in America through their loyalty to Britain during the Revolution. Allan took rooms in Clerkenwell Close, which was fairly conven- ient for Lincoln's Inn Fields, where the Commissioners were sitting. His son James, now twenty-eight and the veteran of campaigns in the Carolinas, was with him. James had no claims of his own to present, but he was there to testify to the truth of his cousin Donald's statements.

Each claimant had to produce witnesses to his loyalty, to his activity on behalf of the government and to the truth of his statements about his possessions. Governor Josiah Martin, General Donald MacDonald and Lord Cornwallis tirelessly swore to the loyalty, the energy, the devotion of their former officers. The claimants all testified that they had visited one another's plantations and had seen the buildings, the furniture, the orchards, the fields, the cattle for which compensation was being asked. It was a reunion of relatives and former neighbors: Alexander MacLeod, Alexander MacDonald of Cuidreach and his son Donald, Allan MacDonald and James, Captain MacDonald of Staten Island, Alexander Morrison of Cross Hill, Murdoch Mac-Leod the surgeon and others. Flora's sister Annabella, Cuidreach's wife, had had harrowing experiences after the defeat of the Highlanders. For as long as she could she stayed at Mt. Pleasant, though the house was frequently plundered. At length with her children she was driven out into the woods, and only the kindness of a captain in the marauding party, who escorted them within the British lines, saved them. Her husband was by that time with Cornwallis in Charles Town; he rewarded the captain with all the cash that he had.

Allan MacDonald filed two claims, in which there are slight differences; one had been sent earlier from Halifax through an agent. The total sums, however, are approximately the same. He valued his two plantations at £400, his gristmill, which, he said, provided bread for the family for a year, at £150; his plate, furniture and books at £500 with £40 off for what Flora managed to salvage, the unexpired terms of his eight indentured servants at £195, his expenses in connection with the Highland uprising at £299.12.11. These included his trips from Anson County to Cape Fear to confer with the Governor; the arms, blankets, shoes and shirts and the cask of rum that he bought for the soldiers; the five horses, the family arms, the saddles and the baggage that were captured after the Battle of Moore's Creek Bridge.[3]

The Commissioners were inclined to regard the accounts

as inflated. No one got anywhere near what he asked for. Allan, writing hopefully, "Your Memorialist expects that the Hon. Board of Commissioners will look to and commisserate the Misfortunes of an old Gentleman worn out with fatigue and service," asked for £1,341, but he got only £440. With this small fruit of his life's adventures and services, he returned to Skye.

He and Flora had been separated for six years; he found a daughter whom he had last seen when she was eight years old now a blooming nineteen. They had no home.

Anne and Alexander MacLeod were at Dunvegan, where they stayed until the chief, by that time a general, returned from India to occupy the castle himself; they then moved to Beg Vaternish.[4] Kingsburgh was still occupied by the same William MacLeod who had taken it in 1774.

Allan and Flora and Fanny continued to visit relatives in the Long Island. They were in South Uist in 1787 when Flora received a letter from her son John, then twenty-eight years old and well started on a distinguished career, the only one of Flora's seven children to become well known in his own right. In 1780 he had won a cadetship in the Bombay Infantry; later, he was transferred to the Bengal Engineers and sent to Sumatra as a surveyor, where he did well and rose to the rank of colonel. He married a young widow, a Mrs. Boyle who died after the birth of her second child. His second wife was the daughter of Dr. Johnson's friend, Sir Robert Chambers, an Indian judge and President of the Asiatic Society, of which John MacDonald was one of the charter members. He retired on half pay at forty-one, lived in Exeter, wrote prolifically and was made a Fellow of the Royal Society. He had seven sons, one of whom he named Charles Edward, and two daughters, and in his later life was known for his charitable activities.

At twenty-eight he wrote:

My dear Mother,

I have just time to tell you that I am recalled to Bengal. I am now proceeding to Prince of Wales Island to Survey the same, and then to Bengal. The vessel waits for this. God bless you and yours. . . . Inform my father of my change of place and my brothers and sisters. I have ordered £1,000 to be given to you immediately for your and Fanny's use and £40 to Anny. I have also ordered two-thirds of the Interest of £1,400 to be given to you annually, and the other one-third to Anny — If Fanny marries with her parents' consent she is to have £100 — My child (handsome to the last degree) her Aunt carries hom this year — she will be better off with her than with any other person as she is rich and fond of her — In her Mother I lost the best of women — I must stop, I am in good health — in 2 months more I will write you.

Your Affectionate son
John MacDonald

On board the Ravensworth Indiaman Streights of Sunda. The London Indiaman carries this, no time to read it over, God bless you.[5]

Charles was in Skye now, married to Isabella MacDonald, a daughter of the MacDonalds of Aird. James had married Emily MacDonald, daughter of the MacDonalds of Heiskir, and had taken her to Flodigarry, where they lived in the house in which Flora and Allan had begun their married life.

In 1789 Flora wrote to Sir John MacPherson, in answer to a request of his, the accounts previously quoted of her experiences with Prince Charles Edward Stuart in 1746 and in North Carolina in the 1770's. Sir John, who had been born in the year of the 'Forty-five, was the son of the minister of Sleat whose Latin verse Dr. Johnson praised in 1774 and the nephew of Donald Roy MacDonald's teacher. Educated at King's College, Aberdeen, and the University of Edinburgh, he went to India, where he had a post in the East India

Company, rose to be Governor General of India, was created
a baronet, was superseded by Lord Cornwallis in 1786 and
returned to England. That he too was a cousin of Flora
MacDonald's seems probable in view of the affectionate
terms of the covering letter which she wrote to accompany
her statements.

To the Honourable Sir John McPherson, late Gove. Gen. of
    India. London.
Honoured Dear Sir:
    Here inclosed the papers you were so very good as to desire
me to send you. I hope they are to the purpose being exact
truth. They are longer than I would wish but shorter I could not
make them. My husband had a letter from my John lately. he was
very ill in his passage from Calcutta to Benevolin for two months
but is now thank God well and on the surveying business. I
need not desire you to mention his name to any of the Directors
you are acquainted with. All friends in this Island are as you left
them and with my husband's blessing who is always tender
with his legs. And my constant prayers to the Almighty to bless,
protect and be your guide and director I am Dr Sir
                     Yours affectionately while able to sign
                              Flora McDonald
Leabost by Sconcer, October 21, 1789
I am always oppressed with the Rheumatism since I saw you.
God bless you.[6]

The body of the letter was written in a different hand
from the signature, and so errors in spelling and punctuation
need not be laid at Flora's door. Her long account of her
experiences first in the 'Forty-five and then in the Rebellion,
she ended on a sad little note:

The cast in both my arms are liveing monuments of my suffer-
ings and distresses. And the long Goal confinement which my
Husband underwent has brought on such disorders that he has

194

totally lost the use of his legs. So that I may fairly say we both have suffered in our person, family and interest, as much as if not more than any two going under the name of Refugees or Loyalists, without the Smallest recompence.

There had been, besides the boatmen, three in the boat that stormy midsummer night in 1746. Charles Edward had died the previous year in Rome, a broken alcoholic of sixty-eight. His wife had left him for another man; Charlotte, Duchess of Albany, his daughter by his mistress Clementina Walkinshaw, would have nothing to do with him. During the forty-two years after his escape from the Highlands, he had never once made any attempt to get in touch with those who had given him aid at the risk of their lives, had sent no message. Neil MacEachain MacDonald, who had managed to avoid capture in Skye, had made his way to the mainland of Scotland, joined Charles and accompanied him to France. There he dropped the MacEachain from his name, joined the French army, married a Frenchwoman, who was quick-tempered, it was said, and a great talker, and produced a son. In 1789 Jacques Étienne Joseph Alexandre MacDonald was thirty-four and a lieutenant in the French army, but in less than twenty years he would be famous as Napoleon Bonaparte's great Marshal MacDonald, Duc de Tarentum.

The Duke of Cumberland had died in 1765 at the age of forty-four, unmarried and enormously fat.

Perhaps Sir John MacPherson, who was at this time Member of Parliament for Cricklade, had suggested to Flora that if he had all the facts of her experiences he might be able to do something for her in London, but if so it came to nothing. Sir John was at about that time unseated on charges of bribery and corruption (apparently unfounded), and Flora herself was soon beyond the need for assistance.

The illness which was shadowed in the letter to Sir John fell on Flora within a few months. She and Allan were visiting friends at Penduin, a tack near Kingsburgh, when she was stricken.[7] She was attended by Dr. John MacLean, the old physician to the MacDonalds who had dressed Donald Roy's foot after Culloden and drawn up the marriage contract for Flora and Allan in 1750. He wrote to his son, Sir Lauchlan MacLean of Surrey, "Nothing has occurred since I wrote you except the death of the famous Mrs. Flora MacDonald, some time of Kingsburgh. She suffered much distress for a long time in my neighborhood at Penduin."[8]

She died on March 4, 1790, and was buried in the burial place of the Kingsburgh MacDonalds at Kilmuir on the coast of Loch Snizort, sixteen miles north of Kingsburgh. Alexander MacGregor wrote that an old man who had been present told him that Flora's funeral was the greatest that had ever been on the island, that the cortege which wound over the hills to Kilmuir was more than a mile long, that a dozen pipers played the coronach and that 300 gallons of whisky were drunk at the feasting afterwards. It might well have been true. Highland funerals were great social occasions, and Flora was famous and much loved.

Later in the year of Flora's death her daughter Fanny, now twenty-four, was married to her cousin Donald, Cuidreach's son, the young planter of Anson County and soldier in Tarleton's Legion, whose character was testified to in the Loyalist Papers with unusual fervor as being "always modest and virtuous." The young couple went to live at first with Donald's parents at Kingsburgh House, for in 1790 the lease became vacant and Alexander MacDonald of Cuidreach was able to get it. Allan, after Flora's death, went to live there too, and in his old home, which he had loved, he died on September 20, 1792, two and a half years after Flora.

Some years later John, after he had come back from India to live in Exeter, raised a monument to his mother at Kilmuir, a slender marble shaft. Within a few months it had disappeared, chipped away bit by bit and carried off as souvenirs by visitors. These were not American tourists — tourism did not yet exist and Skye was a remote place — these were Scottish pilgrims to the grave of a gentle, courageous, steadfast and charming girl who had captured their imaginations and held their affection.

In 1871 a second monument, an Iona cross, a tall stone cross with a circle surrounding the intersection, was erected, and when that was blown down in one of those swift violent gales that lash the Hebrides, a sturdier one was put up which still stands. On it are engraved those words of Dr. Samuel Johnson's, which can not easily be bettered:

"Her name will be mentioned in history, and if courage and fidelity be virtues, mentioned with honor."

NOTES

Notes to Chapter 1

1. Allan Reginald MacDonald, *The Truth about Flora Mac-Donald* (Inverness, 1938), p. 2.
2. Judicial Rental of the Barony of MacDonald. Cited in *Truth*, p. 5.
3. *Truth*, pp. 2–3.
4. William Jolly, *Flora MacDonald in Uist*, in Alexander MacGregor, *The Life of Flora MacDonald* (Stirling, 1932), p. 198.
5. Johnson's *Journey to the Western Islands of Scotland and* Boswell's *Journal of a Tour to the Hebrides*, ed. by R. W. Chapman (Oxford University Press, 1930), p. 91.
6. Robert Forbes, *The Lyon in Mourning* (Scottish History Society, XX, XXI, XXII, Edinburgh, 1895–1897), vol. I, p. 116.
7. The Reverends MacDonald, *Clan Donald* (Inverness, 1896–1904), vol. III, p. 4.
8. Robert Chambers, *Traditions of Edinburgh* (Edinburgh, 1868), pp. 194–195.
9. James Boswell, *Journal of a Tour to the Hebrides with Samuel Johnson*, ed. by Frederick A. Pottle and Charles H. Bennett (New York, 1936), p. 224.
10. Alexander MacGregor, *The Life of Flora MacDonald* (Stirling, 1901), p. 27.
11. *Truth*, p. 2.

Notes to Chapter 2

1. Andrew Lang, *Prince Charles Edward Stuart, the Young Chevalier* (London, 1903), p. 43.
2. A. W. Ward, G. W. Prothero, and Stanley Leathes, eds.,

Cambridge Modern History, vol. VI (Cambridge University Press, 1909), p. 111.

3. P. Hume Brown, *History of Scotland* (Cambridge, 1911), vol. III, p. 292.

4. Alexander Carlyle, *Autobiography, Containing Memorials of the Men and Events of His Time,* 2d. ed. (Edinburgh, 1860), p. 133.

5. Anne Grant, *Letters Written by Mrs. Grant of Laggan Concerning Highland Affairs and Persons Connected with the Stuart Cause in the 18th Century,* ed. by J. R. N. MacPhail (Scottish History Society, 1896), p. 291.

6. *Lyon,* vol. I, p. 304, from the report of John MacKinnon to Mr. Forbes.

7. *The Highlands in 1750,* quoted in Stephen Bone, *The West Coast of Scotland* (London, 1952), p. 8.

8. *Lyon,* vol. I, p. 304.

9. Sir Charles Petrie, *The Stuart Pretenders* (Boston, 1934), p. 188.

10. Carlyle, *Autobiography,* p. 153.

11. Brown, *History of Scotland,* vol. III, p. 324.

12. Sir Charles Petrie, *The Jacobite Movement: the Last Phase, 1716–1807* (London, 1950), p. 111.

13. *Ibid.* p. 109.

14. John Prebble, *Culloden* (New York, 1962), p. 193.

15. *Ibid.* p. 215.

16. *Lyon,* vol. III, p. 97.

17. *Ibid.,* vol. II, p. 99.

18. William Laird Clowes, *The Royal Navy, a History* (London, 1898), vol. III, p. 112.

19. *Lyon,* vol. II, p. 99.

20. Lang, *Prince Charles Edward Stuart,* p. 290.

21. *Lyon,* vol. I, p. 179.

22. Ms. in the National Library of Scotland.

23. *Lyon,* vol. I, p. 80.

24. Walter Biggar Blaikie, ed., *Origins of the 'Forty-five and Other Papers Relating to That Rising* (Scottish History Society, 1916), p. 241.

25. *Ibid.* pp. 249–250.

26. Quoted in Jolly, *Flora MacDonald in Uist,* p. 212.

Notes to Chapter 3

1. Blaikie, *Origins,* lxx.
2. *Lyon,* vol. I, p. 157. Donald MacLeod's account.
3. Ms. in the National Library of Scotland.
4. *Truth,* p. 14.
5. *Lyon,* vol. I, p. 106. O'Neil's Journal.
6. *Ibid.*
7. Blaikie, *Origins,* p. 251. MacEachain's account.
8. *Lyon,* vol. I, p. 106.
9. *Ibid.,* p. 110.
10. *Ibid.,* p. 106.
11. Flora MacDonald to Sir John MacPherson, 1789.
12. *Lyon,* vol. I, p. 296.
13. Blaikie, *Origins,* pp. 252–253.
14. Flora MacDonald to Sir John MacPherson, 1789.
15. Flora MacDonald, Statement at Applecross Bay. Ms. in Public Record Office, London.
16. *Lyon,* vol. I, p. 279. Conversation of Captain John Hay of the Customs House Yacht at Ayr with Mr. Forbes.
17. *Ibid.,* p. 111.
18. Flora MacDonald at Applecross Bay.

Notes to Chapter 4

1. "Over the Sea to Skye." The popular *Skye Boat Song* was written in 1884 by Sir Harold Boulton, to an earlier tune. The chorus and two of the verses follow:

> "Speed bonnie boat, like a bird on the wing,
> Onward," the sailors cry,
> "Carry the lad that's born to be king
> Over the sea to Skye."
>
> Loud the winds howl, loud the waves roar,
> Thunder clouds rend the air;

Baffled our foes stand on the shore,
Follow they would not dare.

Though the waves leap, soft shall ye sleep,
Ocean's a royal bed,
Rocked in the deep, Flora will keep
Watch by your weary head.

2. *Lyon,* vol. I, p. 305.
3. Blaikie, *Origins,* p. 261.
4. *Lyon,* vol. I, p. 305. Actually they were songs of a still earlier time: Charles II was the King, the twenty-ninth of May both his birthday and the day of his Restoration.
5. *Ibid.,* p. 299.
6. Blaikie, *Origins,* p. 261.
7. Flora MacDonald, 1789.
8. Blaikie, *Origins,* pp. 262–263.
9. *Lyon,* vol. II, p. 13.
10. *Ibid.,* p. 17 n.
11. Blaikie, *Origins,* p. 265.
12. *Lyon,* vol. I, p. 117.
13. David Campbell to Mr. Maule, July 21, 1746. State Papers, Scotland, 54:33. Public Record Office, London.
14. Statement of Charles MacNabb, July 9, 1746. Ms. in the National Library of Scotland.
15. *Lyon,* vol. II, pp. 19–21.
16. Donald Roy MacDonald, *Lyon,* vol. II, p. 25; Flora MacDonald, *Lyon,* vol. II, p. 18 n.

Notes to Chapter 5

1. Charles MacNabb.
2. *Lyon,* vol. I, p. 114.
3. State Papers, Scotland, 54: 32 and 33. Public Record Office, London.
4. *Lyon,* vol. I, pp. 123–124.

5. Kingsburgh's statement to General Campbell. Ms. in the National Library of Scotland.

6. *Lyon*, vol. II, p. 31. Charles used the name Thompson as an alias more than once. In 1755–56 he was living at Basel as Mr. D. Thompson.

7. *Ibid.*, vol. I, p. 303.

8. Flora MacDonald's statement, July 12, 1746. State Papers, Scotland, 54:32 and 33. Public Record Office, London.

9. *Lyon*, vol. III, p. 127.

10. *Ibid.*, vol. I, p. 267.

11. *Ibid.*, pp. 110–111.

12. Duncan Forbes, ed., *Culloden Papers* (London, 1815), pp. 290–292.

Notes to Chapter 6

1. *Lyon*, vol. I, p. 113.

2. Ferguson, readers will be relieved to know, came to a bad end. Returning from India to England, as a passenger, in 1773, he got into a quarrel with a Captain Roache and was stabbed. (*Scots Magazine*, January, 1774, p. 54.)

3. *Lyon*, vol. I, p. 115.

4. *Ibid.*, pp. 111–112.

5. Ms. in the National Library of Scotland.

6. Boswell, *Tour*, p. 139.

Notes to Chapter 7

1. *Truth*, p. 67.

2. *Lyon*, vol. II, p. 180.

3. *Ibid.*, p. 178.

4. Petrie, *The Jacobite Movement*, pp. 142–144.

5. *Truth*, p. 76.

6. *Ibid.*, pp. 123–126.

7. *Lyon*, vol. III, p. 81.

Notes to Chapter 8

1. *Truth,* p. 107.
2. Boswell, *Tour,* p. 222.
3. *Truth,* pp. 107–109.
4. *Ibid.,* pp. 110–111.
5. John Pinkerton, ed., *A General Collection of the Best and Most Interesting Voyages and Travels in All Parts of the World* (London, 1809), vol. III, p. 324.

Notes to Chapter 9

1. *Lyon,* vol. III, p. 259.
2. Kingsburgh to MacKenzie of Delvine, April 30, 1771. The National Library of Scotland.
3. I. F. Grant, *The MacLeods: the History of a Clan, 1200–1956* (London, 1959), p. 569.
4. *North Carolina Colonial Records,* vol. IX, p. 303.
5. Ms. in the National Library of Scotland.
6. *Ibid.*
7. Brown, *History of Scotland,* vol. III, p. 77.
8. Ms. in the National Library of Scotland.
9. Boswell, *Tour,* pp. 242–243.

Notes to Chapter 10

1. Boswell, *Tour,* p. 154 n.
2. *Ibid.,* p. 159. Though Johnson had received an honorary doctorate from Dublin in 1765, he did not have one from Oxford till 1775, and even Boswell was still calling him Mr. in 1773.
3. *The Letters of Samuel Johnson,* with Mrs. Thrale's genuine letters to him, collected and edited by R. W. Chapman (Oxford, 1952), Vol. I, p. 363.
4. Johnson, *Journey,* p. 60.

Notes

Notes to Chapter 11

1. *Truth*, pp. 110–111.
2. *Ibid.*, p. 97.
3. Boswell, *Tour*, p. 156.
4. Janet Schaw, *Journal of a Lady of Quality*, being a Narrative of a Journey from Scotland to the West Indies, North Carolina and Portugal in the Years 1774–1776, ed. by Evangeline Walker Andrews in collaboration with Charles McLean Andrews (New Haven, 1927), pp. 52–53.

Notes to Chapter 12

1. J. P. MacLean, *Flora MacDonald in America* (Lumberton, N.C., 1909), p. 32.
2. Schaw, *Journal*, p. 281.
3. Loyalist Papers, A.O. Class 12, vols. 36, 99, 109, Class 13, Bundle 121, Public Record Office, London.
4. William Henry Foote, *Sketches of North Carolina* (New York, 1846), pp. 155, 156.
5. Loyalist Papers.

Notes to Chapter 13

1. Loyalist Papers. Transcript in New York Public Library, vol. 45, p. 73.
2. Robert DeMond, *The Loyalists in North Carolina During the Revolution* (Durham, N.C., 1960), p. 65.
3. Loyalist Papers, Public Record Office.
4. Schaw, *Journal*, p. 281.
5. Duane Meyer, *The Highland Scots of North Carolina 1732–1776* (Raleigh, 1963), p. 64.
6. *N. C. Colonial Records*, vol. X, p. 47.
7. Ms. in Public Record Office, AO 13/121.

8. *N. C. Colonial Records*, vol. X, p. 65.
9. *Ibid.*, p. 125.
10. Loyalist Papers.
11. *Ibid.* Also *N. C. Colonial Records*, vol. X, p. 325: The Governor wrote to Lord Dartmouth Nov. 12, 1775: "The taking away these Gentlemen from this Province will in a great measure if not totally dissolve the union of the Highlanders in it now held together by their influence."
12. *N. C. Colonial Records*, vol. X, p. 299.

Notes to Chapter 14

1. *N. C. Colonial Records*, vol. X, pp. 441–442.
2. Hugh F. Rankin, "The Moore's Creek Bridge Campaign," in *North Carolina Historical Review*, vol. XXX (Jan. 1953), p. 34.
3. *N. C. Colonial Records*, vol. X, p. 326.
4. Foote, *Sketches*, p. 490.
5. Loyalist Papers.
6. Letter from an unknown source, dated March 10, 1776, in *N. C. Colonial Records*, pp. 485–486.
7. DeMond, *Loyalists in North Carolina*, p. 97.

Notes to Chapter 15

1. Flora MacDonald to Sir John MacPherson, 1789.
2. Peter Force, ed., *American Archives* (Washington, 1844), ser. 4, vol. V., p. 1346.
3. Alexander MacDonald, *Letter-book* (New York Historical Society *Collections*, 1882), p. 387.
4. Loyalist Papers.
5. *N. C. State Records*, vol. XIII, pp. 56–57.
6. *Ibid.*, pp. 64–65.
7. Loyalist Papers.

Notes

Notes to Chapter 16

1. Force, *American Archives*, ser. 4, vol. VI, p. 613.
2. *Ibid.*, ser. 5, vol. II, p. 192.
3. *N. C. Colonial Records*, vol. XI, pp. 295–296.
4. John Ferdinand Dalziel Smith, quoted in C. C. Crittenden, *The Commerce of North Carolina, 1763–1789* (New Haven, 1936), p. 21.
5. *N. C. Colonial Records*, vol. XI, pp. 295–296.
6. Force, *American Archives*, ser. 4, vol. VI, p. 614.
7. W. C. Ford, *Journals of the Continental Congress, 1774–1789*, vol. XI, p. 248.
8. Edmund Cody Burnett, *The Continental Congress* (New York, 1941), pp. 191 ff.
9. Ford, *Journals*, vol. XI, p. 385.
10. Petition of Captain Allan MacDonald of Kingsburgh, April 5, 1777, in *Papers of the Continental Congress, 1774–1789*, no. 42, vol. V, folio 41.
11. Letter to Alexander Bartram, merchant in Market Street, Philadelphia. Ms. in Library of the Pennsylvania Historical Society.
12. *Papers of the Continental Congress*, no. 78, vol. XV, folio 231.
13. MacDonald, *Letter-book*, pp. 377–378.
14. *Ibid.*, pp. 388–389.
15. *Ibid.*, p. 394.
16. *Ibid.*, p. 401.

Notes to Chapter 17

1. Flora MacDonald to Sir John MacPherson, 1789.
2. MacDonald, *Letter-book*, p. 441.
3. Letter, 1789.
4. MacDonald, *Letter-book*, pp. 484–485.
5. Letter, 1789.

6. *Ibid.*
7. *Ibid.*
8. *Truth,* p. 111.
9. *Ibid.,* p. 95.

Notes to Chapter 18

1. *Truth,* p. 95.
2. Ms. in the National Library of Scotland.
3. Loyalist Papers.
4. "Flora MacDonald at Dunvegan Castle," in *Clan MacLeod Magazine,* II (1953), p. 94.
5. *Truth,* p. 112.
6. Ms. in the National Library of Scotland. The name of the place from which the letter was written has previously been read Seabost, but Dr. Donald MacKinnon tells me that the initial S should be read L and that Leabost is near Kingsburgh.
7. "Flora MacDonald at Dunvegan Castle," p. 96.
8. *Truth,* p. 98.